T0054381

XOOT

The Inherent Judaism in String Theory

—

ACKNOWLEDGMENTS

Special Thanks To

My parents, Dr Amiel & Dr Edna Tokayer, who instilled in me Jewish values and understandings through being excellent examples of living life well.

The Chabad-Lubavitch family of FAU: Rabbi Baruch Shmuel and Rebbetzin Rivka Rochel Liberow and their many children, who perfectly exemplify what it means to be Chabad.

My sister, Eliana Tokayer, for improving the coherence of this book through listening to and organizing my often-insane ramblings.

Sasha Lutz for her incredibly insightful commentary on the initial clarity of this work.

And Rivka Reich for her fantastic cover illustration.

Additional Thanks To

My siblings: Jake, Tai, Kiwi, & Eliana.

All those who wished to remain anonymous.

And all who helped in the production of this work.

TABLE OF CONTENTS

INTRODUCTION

This work is divided into five sections:

1: A History of Math.

We must understand the history of math and how it works through logic.

2: String Theory

String Theory is the modern pinnacle of physics. Since it is incredibly complex, to develop an understanding, we must first understand the basics: why we have String Theory and what generally makes it work. Then, we learn about concepts that are different from our normal understanding of physics. Only then can we learn the nature of String Theory, slowly moving into more difficult subsections that are increasingly math intensive.

3: Judaism

Orthodox Judaism, a branch of Judaism, firmly believes in monotheism, rejecting the idea of multiple gods. Within its rationalist framework, there's a clear distinction between priorities, whether they be rituals or prayers. This important argument fostered a logical understanding of Jewish principles, nurturing the development of scientific reasoning, especially after the denominational split between Orthodox & Reform. Interestingly, Hasidism (a denomination of Orthodox Judaism), despite its limited scientific knowledge, echoes certain modern scientific consensus views through its various additions to Judaic practices. As a whole, Judaism emphasizes the concept of everything being interconnected within one divine entity, highlighting the fundamental nature of our connection to it. By applying mathematical axioms rooted in Orthodox Jewish principles, we can observe how the logical structure of Judaism aligns with modern mathematical logic and the overall connection between the two fields.

4: Xoot

These two theories of everything are the same. From the simple, conceptual parallels, we can understand the fascinating overlap. Correlation does not necessarily mean causation, but in this case, (a) one does not affect the other. They are both the same. And (b) studying the correlation is a necessary first step to understand the underlying fundamental connection. We prove this connection through the logic in both of them.

5: Ideation

A random assortment of some of my personal opinions and reasoned deductions.

The first section, A History of Math, naturally leads into the second section, String Theory. String Theory and the third section, Judaism, are needed to understand Xoot, the fourth section. The final section, Ideation, is a bonus section that is completely separate from the other four sections.

A HISTORY OF MATH

Euclid

In 300 BCE, the Greek mathematician, Euclid, attempted to summarize all mathematical logic known at the time. People's logical trains went in circles, so Euclid wanted to prove that all math boils down to a few indisputable rules (commonly known as *postulates* when it comes to Euclid and *axioms* when it comes to everything else). If we believe these rules to be true, then we can build theorems based on those rules and theorems based on other already-proven theorems. We can even prove that these rules work through the other rules. If the rules are true, then everything that is logically based on those rules must also be true. He began with definitions of the terms used in the rules:

Some of Euclid's definitions:

1. A point is something that has no part.

2. A line is a breadthless length.

3. The ends of the lines are points.

4. A straight line is a line which lies evenly within the points on itself.

Euclid derived four postulates:

1. If you have two points, you can draw a straight line between them.

2. If you have a straight line, you can extend it infinitely.

3. If you have a center and a radius, you can draw a circle.

4. All right-angles are equal.

He then derived a complicated postulate:

5. If a straight line that intersects with two straight lines makes the interior angles on the same side less than two right angles, then if you extend the two straight lines infinitely, the two straight lines will meet on the side in which the interior angles are less than two right angles.

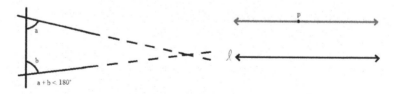

web.colby.edu - The Geometric Viewpoint | History of Hyperbolic Geometry

This fifth postulate confused other mathematicians. It's not simple and blatantly obvious, like the others. It seems to be a theorem itself, not a basic rule of geometry. (If you're Jewish, then

14

you'll likely understand this confusion through the following phrase: Mah Nishtana Ha*Postulate* Hazeh).

If the fifth rule is a theorem, that means it can be proven using the four other rules. Mathematicians tried to come up with a different fifth postulate, but any "new" postulate was either a restatement or wouldn't logically work. It could not be done. The fifth postulate only allows for **one** line that intersects with a specific point to parallel a different line. If you tried to prove that **zero** straight lines through a point can parallel a different straight line, you would need to pretend that either parallel lines don't exist or the second postulate is wrong, which doesn't make sense. If you tried to prove that **more than one** straight line, passing through the same point, can be parallel to another straight line, the math actually works out, but things get a bit crazy.

The Search For Impossible Geometry

János Bolyai, a Hungarian mathematician, worked out that, contrary to Euclid's understanding, you can have more than one straight line pass through the same point and all be parallel to another straight line. If you tried to draw this out on paper, it fails, but that's not because Bolyai's work is wrong.

The paper is wrong.

The paper is trying to represent our three-dimensional world in two dimensions, but nobody said the rules and logic of our world must be defined on only flat (two dimensional) surfaces. Imagine a hyperbolic geometric shape, like a saddle, and on this shape, there is a straight line called AB. You can, on a hyperbolic shape, draw a point and get more than one straight line to pass through that point and be parallel to AB. From a top-down perspective, these new lines may not look straight, but from the surface of the shape, they are.

Mathematician Carl Gauss noted that this supposed proof of what he called Non-Euclidean geometry was the same as Gauss's own work that Gauss didn't publish because he thought the world would initially reject this idea and harm him, just like any scientist or mathematician who disagreed with the local church at the time.

It was later understood that the geometry of spheres is another type of geometry that works mathematically, but doesn't allow for any parallel lines. In this case, we wouldn't have to worry about the second postulate not holding up because by extending a straight line far enough around a circle, it loops back and connects to itself, which acts as an infinitely long straight line[1].

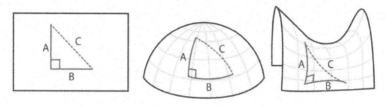

drmarkliu.com - Non-Euclidian – Dr. Mark Liu

Euclidean and Non-Euclidean geometries work because they're based on postulates which are based on Euclid's definitions, but there's a problem.

The Problem With Definitions

What does it mean to "have a part"?

What does it mean to have "breadth"?

None of these specific terms are defined, and even if they were, those new definitions would use terms that need to be defined, and you can't have a functioning understanding of the universe if every term used is defined by other terms. If you allow terms to be defined, then your understanding of the universe is based on an infinite series of going back-and-forth between definitions. In this sense,

---

[1] Refining the second postulate is credited to Bernhard Riemann.

Euclid fell into the same trap as the rest of the mathematicians of his time.

You should instead have, as Professor Alex Kontorovich[2] explains, "*undefined terms. I'm not gonna [have to] tell you what a point is. I'm not gonna [have to] tell you what a line is... All I'm gonna have to tell you is what the postulates are that [these undefined terms] are assumed to satisfy. It's the relationships between the objects that's important... And then four of those axioms are satisfied, just not the fifth*" (Lewis).

If we drop the definitions and just keep the first four postulates, then our understanding improves.

In geometry, the fifth postulate has a relationship that's different from the other postulates. The four others work perfectly fine regardless of the structure of the universe. The fifth defines the structure of the universe. (**We see this same type of relationship appear in the first chapter of String Theory**)

The Geometry of the Universe

Albert Einstein used these four postulates as a basis for creating two more: the laws of physics are the same regardless of one's reference frame, and the speed of light is the same for all inertial observers. Therefore, space and time must be relative, and, since gravity was originally defined (by Isaac Newton) as a force from a universal reference frame, that understanding of gravity must be wrong. Instead, Einstein explained that gravity is not a force, but a function of the stretching and squeezing of spacetime, affecting the geometry of the universe. Speaking of, what is the geometry of the universe? Does it follow Euclidean, spherical, or hyperbolic geometry?

---

[2] *In a YouTube video from the channel Veritasium. "How One Line in the Oldest Math Text Hinted at Hidden Universes"*

How many lines can pass through a single point and still be parallel to a different (straight) line?

A. If the universe has no parallel lines, then you're on a sphere, and the angles of the triangle should be more than 180-degrees.

B. If the universe can do that with one parallel line, it's flat, and the angles of the triangle should be exactly 180 degrees.

C. If the universe can do that with more than one, it's hyperbolic, and the angles of the triangle should be less than 180 degrees.

The triangle (that we should use to measure which type of geometry our universe is) should be large enough relative to the size of the universe that the effects of curvature become prominent, like the difference between drawing a small triangle on a globe and one that connects the top to the middle. The small triangle essentially operates as if it's on a flat surface within a small rounding error, whereas the larger triangle notably operates with spherical geometry. So, let's use the biggest structure in our universe, the Cosmic Microwave Background Radiation (CMBR).

Looking at it indicates that there are pockets of hotter radiation and spots of colder radiation. If we can analyze the true size of any of these spots, we can draw a triangle with one corner as the observer (us), one corner as the top of the spot, and one corner as the bottom of the spot. Each spot was independently analyzed and organized from hottest to coldest.

The study found that our universal triangle had a total angle size of nearly 180 degrees, with the overall curvature of the universe to be within the margin of error.

Our universe is flat.

And we don't know why. If the average density of the universe was increased or decreased by a few atoms for every desk-sized piece of space, then we would need to use the math of spherical or hyperbolic geometry to describe the universe on a literal universal scale. Our universe, according to classical physics, happens to exist within the simplest third-dimensional geometry, making the math of classical physics relatively simple.

This would be our understanding of the universe if it wasn't for the weirdness of the quantum world.

STRING THEORY

String Theory is the modern pinnacle of physics. Since it is incredibly complex, to develop an understanding, we must first understand the basics: why we have String Theory and what generally makes it work. Then, we learn about concepts that are different from our normal understanding of physics. Only then can we learn the nature of String Theory, slowly moving into more difficult subsections that are increasingly math intensive.

—

The Basics

Let's count to 4.

One, two, three, gravity.

One universe, two sets of rules, three forces guiding our universe, and gravity.

Within the one universe, there are two sets of rules: the rules that everything above the size of an atom follows, and the rules that everything smaller than an atom follows. Scientifically, we thought that everything obeys the laws of physics, but from what we've learned about things that are smaller than an atom is that things in the sub-atomic world operate differently. Things appear from nothing and disappear into nothing. Things exist in two places at once. Things move and stop in ways that don't make sense in the normal world. In fact, the entire idea of the famous Schrodinger's Cat experiment was to prove that the mechanics of the subatomic (quantum) world and the physics of our world don't mesh - the cat is both alive and dead. Everything smaller than an atom follows a different set of rules called quantum mechanics, instead of normal (classical) physics.

If we want to truly understand the universe, we have to know what the really real rules of the universe are - rules that make sense from both the normal (classical physics) world and the subatomic (quantum mechanical) world. So, if you're feeling social, let's meet some of these rules. I dub these the "easy three".

1. Electromagnetism

Electromagnetism is this cool force that brings electricity and magnets together, showing how they're connected in the universe. You can use magnets to make electricity and amp up magnetic fields with electric currents. Back in the day, people were debating what light really is. As it turns out, it's kind of like a mixed bag – sometimes it acts like tiny particles called photons, and other times it acts like a wave. The length of each wave - its wavelength - stretches across this spectrum: you've got radio waves with the longest wavelength, then microwaves, infrared, visible light (the rainbow colors), ultraviolet, X-rays, and gamma rays.

Electromagnetism follows this rule where opposite stuff attracts - opposites attract and sames repulse. So, positive and negative charges, or those magnetic poles, are all about coming together because of this force. Basically, electromagnetism shows how electricity and magnets are like two peas in a pod, always sticking together and making things happen in the universe.

2. The Strong Force

The strong nuclear force, also known as the strong interaction or nuclear strong force acts within the nucleus of an atom. It is responsible for binding together protons and neutrons, the building blocks of atomic nuclei, despite their electric charges and the repulsive electromagnetic force between positively charged protons.

The strong nuclear force is an extremely powerful force that operates over very short distances within the nucleus, on the order of a few femtometers. (0.00000000000001 meters)

It is the strongest of the four fundamental forces, much stronger than the electromagnetic force, which governs the interactions between charged particles. Unlike the electromagnetic force, which decreases with distance, the strong force does not diminish with distance beyond a certain point. Instead, it remains constant within the range of its effective distance, only dropping off sharply beyond that range. This unique property allows it to overcome the electrostatic repulsion (opposites attract and sames repulse) between protons, which are positively charged. The electrostatic repulsion would otherwise cause nuclei to fly apart. So because of the strong force, atoms with more than one proton can be held together.

Protons and neutrons are made of quarks. These quarks are held together by special particles that glue quarks together, called gluons. The exchange of gluons between quarks glues the quarks together, and this creates a complicated web of interactions that bind protons and neutrons together in the nucleus. The strong nuclear force is a fundamental force of nature that binds protons and neutrons together in atomic nuclei, overcoming the electrostatic repulsion between positively charged protons. It operates over extremely short distances and is mediated by gluons, making it the strongest force known in the universe.

3. The Weak Force

The weak force is responsible for certain types of nuclear decay processes and plays a crucial role in the behavior of subatomic particles. At its core, the weak nuclear force is involved in the transformation of one type of particle into another within the nucleus of an atom.

One way the weak force often changes particles is through beta decay. When a neutron takes part in the exchange of certain bosons, the neutron doesn't feel comfortable being neutral anymore and transitions to a proton. This process produces some energy, which results in the release of an electron. The entire process is called beta decay. The electron, called a beta particle, is released. This electron takes away some of the energy from the decay. We see this release of the electron as beta radiation.

Despite its crucial role in nuclear processes, the weak nuclear force is the least powerful of the fundamental forces. Its effects are typically only observed at the subatomic level, within the nucleus of atoms. However, even though it is the weakest force, it still has a significant impact on the behavior and stability of matter in the universe.

These "easy three" are a part of the standard model of particle physics, and work hand-in-hand with our understanding of the world around us. If we understand that everything in the universe works through microscopic particles, it all makes sense.

With the advancement of scientific knowledge, humanity has harnessed the potent force of electromagnetism, which permeates virtually every facet of modern technology. From the intricate workings of electronic devices to the generation of electric power, the influence of electromagnetism is omnipresent in our daily lives.

Through groundbreaking research and the development of projects like the Manhattan Project, humanity has uncovered the formidable capabilities of the strong nuclear force. Yes, the force that governs the interactions between subatomic particles within atomic nuclei has been instrumental in harnessing nuclear energy for non-peaceful purposes and for averting the devastating potential of global conflict.

The weak nuclear force, while the least powerful of the fundamental forces, plays a vital role in various aspects of scientific inquiry and technological applications. It facilitates the proper analysis of physical data, contributes to the precision of timekeeping mechanisms, and finds myriad other uses in fields ranging from particle physics to medical imaging.

In essence, each of these fundamental forces—electromagnetism, the strong nuclear force, and the weak nuclear force—has profoundly shaped the trajectory of human progress and technological advancement, underscoring the importance of scientific exploration and discovery in our quest to understand the workings of the universe.

These are the good guys.

But there's an elephant in the room. The bad guy who doesn't get along with any of the good guys. He interacts with them, but is so fundamentally different from all of them that he can't ever seem to work alongside them. Scientists have used this bad guy alone to progress our understanding of the universe, and yet, he still doesn't fit with the good guys. Maybe he's just different and shouldn't be defined like the others, or maybe he's just like the others and the fact that we think he's different is confusing us. Regardless, his name is gravity, and he had a rough upbringing.

Gravity was born as a headline force.

Isaac Newton originally defined gravity through his work, *Philosophiæ Naturalis Principia Mathematica*, stating that gravity is a force that interacts with stuff by moving it. In the standard model of particle physics, if gravity is a force, it's fundamentally a particle, just like the "easy three".

27

But gravity grew up as a background actor.

Albert Einstein edited this understanding through his theories of general relativity and special relativity, stating that the speed of light is constant. And if the speed of light doesn't change, space and time have to bend instead. Whenever space bends, time bends the same amount consistently, so Einstein called the universal background of space and time *spacetime*. Einstein described gravity as the curvature of spacetime, not as a force. Imagine spacetime as a fabric, and when objects with mass, like planets or stars, sit on this fabric, they cause it to bend or curve. Other objects then move along the curves created by this bending, kind of like how marbles roll along a stretched-out sheet. Gravity, according to the theory of general relativity, is the bending and stretching of the universal background called spacetime. That means it's not based on particles, so it's not a force.

When scientists try to merge the ideas of quantum mechanics with Einstein's theory of general relativity to describe gravity on a small scale, they run into problems because the mathematics and concepts of quantum mechanics and general relativity don't easily mesh together.

The big issue is that quantum mechanics suggests that space and time are not continuous, smooth entities, but rather they're made up of tiny, discrete units - everything is made of particles. This conflicts with the smooth, background picture of spacetime that general relativity presents. If gravity was consistent classically and quantum mechanically, we would have an easy four. The easy three work through both quantum mechanics and classical physics: you can use a mirror to reflect light, you can detonate a nuclear bomb, and you feel the heat of radioactivity, but our only practical physical interaction with gravity is falling. Combining the two different understandings of gravity is not impossible, but very very difficult. Scientists have been working on a theory that can reconcile these differences and describe gravity on both large and small scales, and this is where theories like String Theory come into play. They attempt to provide a framework that can unify gravity with the other fundamental forces in a way that's consistent with both quantum mechanics and general relativity.

This is the gist of String Theory

Imagine you have a group of a special kind of string that can wiggle and vibrate in different ways. Now, these strings move around in spacetime. Spacetime is like the stage where all the action in the universe happens. And as these strings wiggle and vibrate, they create different particles, like electrons, quarks, and photons. Thus, spacetime itself is a surface, just like in our understanding of gravity, and the strings create particles, just like in our understanding of quantum mechanics and the "easy three". Everything works!

However, combining the "easy three" with a spacetime background seems like it solves the issue of the bad guy, but it doesn't work out. After all, the "easy three" is based on the principle that everything in the universe is fundamentally based on particles, so it doesn't make sense to have another force that's entirely based on the structure of the universe. Yet, gravity seems to be a force that's only based on the structure of the universe.

In String Theory, everything is made up of tiny strings that vibrate and move. These vibrations create particles, which are the building blocks of our world. In String Theory, gravity, too, is made from these particles. So, gravity is a fourth fundamental rule of the universe, alongside the "easy three". Gravity isn't just an outsider or background in the universe's rulebook. It's actually one of the fundamental rules. The difference between it and the easy three is that even though the particles that make up gravity are created by tiny vibrating strings, these specific gravity-particles warp spacetime itself. These infinitesimal ripples in spacetime on the smallest scales eventually become enormous waves on the largest scales, affecting how our universe behaves.

So, if, in other theories of the universe, gravity is the bending and stretching of the fabric of spacetime, but in String Theory, gravity is the just particles that stretch spacetime, then, according to String Theory, what is spacetime? What makes up the background fabric of the universe that is bent and stretched by gravity-related particles?

The strings, specifically, when the strings move from one place to another. Yes, those fundamental strings (that vibrate to create the particles that become the forces of the universe) are the very fabric of the universe as well. Here me out:

In general relativity, gravity is based on the large-scale and small-scale bending of spacetime. In String Theory, everything is based on the strings, and since the strings are spacetime, each one of the fundamental forces ("easy three") is fundamentally based on spacetime. Similar to the old debate as to whether light is a particle or a wave, the modern debate is whether gravity is a particle or based on spacetime. And just like the old light debate, String Theory says it's both.

The reasoning is that if strings are spacetime and those strings create particles that act as the fundamental forces of the universe, then gravity is both (a) based on particles and (b) a function of spacetime. When the strings vibrate, that creates particles, but when the strings move, that creates the fabric that we can call spacetime. These strings are so small that just one by itself doesn't do much. When groups of gravity-related particles come together and interact, they tug on spacetime and bend it, affecting things on a bigger scale, eventually moving stars, planets, and galaxies. Overall, certain vibrations of the strings create certain particles that affect spacetime; the process of which influences large-scale structures.

Finding out more about the rules of the fundamental strings can help us understand how our universe works. Let's learn some laws of these strings to find out how they act and explain some of the oddities of their existence.

String Law:

One of these rules is called "conformal symmetry," which means that no matter how the string wiggles and bends, it still looks the same at different points in time and space.

Also, we have even more dimensions - hidden ones that are curled up and impossible to see from the classical physics perspective. These dimensions are like extra layers in spacetime, and they play a big role in how the strings move and interact.

Now, imagine we have two different sets of rules for our strings. One set might describe the strings as dancing in one way, and the other set describes them dancing in a different way. Sometimes, these two sets of rules are actually the same thing in disguise. This is called "duality," where two seemingly different ways of looking at things turn out to be secretly connected.

Advanced String Law:

These strings can oscillate in different modes, giving rise to various particle properties such as mass and charge. The equations describing the motion of these strings are called the "string equations of motion" and are derived from the principles of both quantum mechanics and general relativity. This requires more than the usual three spatial dimensions and one time dimension of our everyday experience. These additional compactified dimensions are curled up or "hidden" at scales smaller than those currently detectable. The mathematical framework for dealing with these extra dimensions involves concepts from differential geometry and topology.

String theory predicts the outcomes of particle collisions, or scattering amplitudes, by summing over all possible ways that strings can interact. The mathematics involved in calculating these scattering amplitudes is intricate and often relies on sophisticated techniques from quantum field theory, as well as mathematical structures such as Riemann surfaces and modular forms.

String theory exhibits various symmetries and dualities, which relate seemingly different physical theories to each other. These symmetries often manifest themselves in surprising mathematical relationships, such as mirror symmetry and T-duality. Exploring these symmetries has led to profound insights into the structure of string theory and its connections to other areas of physics and mathematics.

When we look at string theory in certain situations where the energy is low, we can describe it really well using something called conformal field theories (CFTs). Conformal symmetry is like a special rulebook that helps us understand how things stay the same even when we change their size or shape. Conformal field theories are like special kinds of math that stay the same even if we stretch or rotate them. They're really useful for studying strings, especially when they're not interacting very strongly. So basically, they're like a super helpful toolbox for figuring out what's going on with strings in different situations.

This entire section consists of using advanced string law to explain string law. We began with the introduction of the issue of merging gravity with the three other fundamental forces, then introduced String Theory and how it solves the issue conceptually. We then introduced the idea that strings follow a set of rules. This entire String Theory section of this book is expounding on advanced string law:

We first establish the concepts that don't work in classical physics (such as extra dimensions, duality, and symmetry). We then move into a slightly more complicated understanding of what happens when strings interact with each other (through scattering amplitudes). This has some math, but explained simply.

What makes String Theory work is string movement beyond vibrating. String movement is math intensive and complicated, so it is divided into three chapters, and made simple enough that someone with an understanding of high-school algebra should understand it. The first chapter (Conformal Field Theory) sets the stage of what math we use and how we learn from it. The next chapter (quantization) divides string movement into bite-size pieces, and the final chapter (Stringematics) is a deep dive on string movement through the string equations of motion.

—

Extra Dimensions

How many right-angles can a triangle have? If you said no more than one, you'd be right. This is how we normally think of the universe. We naturally use Euclidean geometry to analyze stuff in a two-dimensional space and we can't understand how there could possibly be a triangle with more than one right-angle, so let's do an experiment. Find a perfect sphere. It could be a globe or a ball. Now, on the sphere, draw a right-angle. Extend both the lines that are connected at the right-angle. Then, for each line, draw a right-angle that creates a line toward the other line. If the right-angles are drawn correctly, you'd have a triangle with three right-angles.

"That's cheating", you might say. "No triangle on a flat surface has more than one right-angle." You're right, but in the context of string theory, we don't use two-dimensional flat surfaces. We use the flat and curved surfaces of our three-dimensional world. In analyzing the curved surfaces of our world, normal Euclidean geometry (the math that says we can't have a three-right-angled triangle) isn't good enough. We switch to differential geometry, which extends the rules of Euclidean geometry to more general curved spaces. Differential geometry allows us to define distances, angles, and shapes on curved spaces, which is essential for understanding how our world behaves in String Theory, and, as you may have guessed from the title of this chapter, how the extra 23 dimensions behave in string theory.

Compactification

Take a piece of paper, put it on a table, and, starting from the top left corner, label all four corners: A, B, C, & D in a clockwise manner. With a little push, you could roll a ball from one corner to another. Now, fold the paper so A & B are touching and C & D are touching. You should have one corner AB and another corner CD along with two other corners. Name the unnamed top corner E. If you were to roll a ball from E to AB, how would that look from the perspective of an unfolded paper?

It would look like the ball started halfway between A & B, then somehow split into two balls - each one moving closer to A & B respectively. From the perspective of the two-dimensional paper, rolling the ball from E to AB broke the rules of classical physics, even though it's just a ball moving in a straight line.

We were able to break the rules of two-dimensional classical physics because we folded the two-dimensional paper through our three-dimensional world. The paper doesn't have depth; we do.

So, if someone were to fold a three-dimensional object through a four-dimensional world, things in the four-dimensional world would appear to break our three-dimensional laws of physics, but those things are simply moving normally through the four-dimensional world. That's how String Theory explains how the laws of quantum mechanics can be different from classical physics. When things in the subatomic world act in three dimensions, classical laws of physics apply, but when the strings interact with higher dimensions, simple interactions in higher dimensions become much more complicated interactions in our dimension, which explains the weirdness of quantum mechanics.

String theory suggests that there are extra dimensions beyond what we normally experience, but they're curled up or compactified so small that we can't see them in our everyday lives. If these extra dimensions were big enough to interact visibly with us, everyday actions like throwing a ball could lead to strange disappearances into higher dimensions. So, these extra dimensions don't appear to directly impact anything larger than an atom. These dimensions are hidden from our usual perception but still impact how strings behave at very small scales or high energies. One way scientists deal with this compactification is by using special shapes called Calabi-Yau manifolds. Think of these as playgrounds where the strings of string theory can move around. These manifolds have unique properties that make them perfect for the strings to curl up on. Essentially, the extra dimensions are hidden within the complex shapes of the Calabi-Yau manifold.

The sizes and shapes of these extra dimensions affect the physical properties and the types of particles we observe in our universe. How the strings vibrate and interact in our dimensions depends on the shape of the Calabi-Yau manifold they're dancing on. Different shapes lead to different patterns of vibration, which correspond to the different particles and forces we see. The complex topology of these manifolds is crucial for understanding how our universe works at low energies. It doesn't seem to change much in these low-energy states, so that's when we study it, but when things get really energetic or tiny, the extra dimensions start to influence the strings by affecting the Calabi-Yau manifold itself.

Compactification involves reducing the number of dimensions of spacetime from the full ten (in the case of superstring theory) or

26 (in the case of bosonic string theory) to a lower number, typically four in order to match our observable universe. This process is essential for connecting string theory to our observed reality. The math used for compactification involves considering how the extra dimensions are curled up or compactified into tiny, nearly invisible shapes called manifolds.

These compact dimensions can take various shapes (such as tori or Calabi-Yau manifolds), each with its own geometry. Mathematically, compactification is described by specifying the metric (a mathematical representation of distances and angles) on the compact dimensions. This metric determines the shape of the compact manifold. In the context of string theory, the compactification process involves finding solutions to the equations of motion and constraints of the theory in the reduced-dimensional spacetime.

The key mathematical tools used in compactification include differential geometry, algebraic geometry, and topology. Differential geometry deals with smooth manifolds and curvature, which are crucial for describing the geometry of spacetime and compact dimensions. Algebraic geometry provides techniques for studying the solutions of equations arising from compactification, particularly in the case of Calabi-Yau compactifications. Topology is important for understanding the global structure of the compact manifold and its implications for physical phenomena.

Overall, the math involved in compactification is highly sophisticated and relies on advanced techniques from differential geometry, algebraic geometry, and topology. It involves solving differential equations and studying the properties of geometric shapes to understand how the extra dimensions are curled up and how they affect the physics observed in our four-dimensional spacetime.

—

Universal Theory

String Theory is not just one understanding. There are many theories that operate within the framework of strings. At any point in this chapter, if you see the phrase "multiple string theories", don't panic. Each String Theory attempts to mathematically explain a principle of the physical world. This entire chapter is logically demonstrating that these "multiple string theories" are actually part of one cohesive theory, and it follows this train of logic:

Leaves are the different string theories, branches are the combination of those theories into aspects of String Theory, and the trunk combines these aspects into one theory.

Duality is the understanding that two seemingly different physical principles are part of the same principle, like how tree leaves meet at branches. In our case, the one principle that was

38

formed from two seemingly different principles is actually one aspect of String Theory. Once we understand that many different physical theories can be narrowed down to a few aspects of String Theory, symmetry connects these aspects into one unified understanding, like how our branches meet at the trunk.

Duality refers to the idea that different physical theories may be equivalent to each other under certain transformations. These transformations can involve exchanging certain quantities or parameters, such as the strength of a force or the shape of space. For example, in String Theory, there is a type of duality called T-duality, which relates string theories in different spacetime backgrounds that have certain geometric properties. This means that two seemingly different theories can describe the same physical phenomena, providing different perspectives on the same underlying reality.

Symmetry, on the other hand, refers to a property of a system that remains unchanged under certain transformations. In the context of String Theory, symmetries can manifest as mathematical operations that leave the equations describing the theory invariant. For example, rotational symmetry means that the laws of physics remain the same under rotations of the coordinate system. In String Theory, there are various symmetries, including spacetime symmetries like Lorentz symmetry (which relates different inertial reference frames) and internal symmetries (which involve transformations within the internal structure of strings).

Both duality and symmetry play important roles in String Theory. They help physicists understand the underlying unity of different physical theories and provide powerful tools for solving problems and making predictions. By studying the symmetries and dualities of String Theory, researchers can uncover deeper insights into the fundamental nature of reality and potentially even develop a unified theory of all the forces in the universe.

At its core, duality in String Theory asserts that different formulations of the theory can be equivalent under certain transformations. This equivalence suggests that the theory remains unchanged despite swapping specific properties or parameters. Two prominent manifestations of duality within String Theory are T-Duality and S-Duality.

Imagine you have two different maps of the same place, but one is zoomed in and the other is zoomed out. T-Duality is like saying that if you take the small-map universe and zoom out really far, it's just like the big-map universe. It's like changing your perspective but still seeing the same things. Then there's S-Duality, which is a bit fancier. It's like saying if you have a super-strong magnet, it acts the same as a super-weak magnet if you look at it in a special way. So, even though the strong and weak magnets seem different, they're kind of secretly the same thing.

T & S

T-Duality, short for Target Space Duality, is this cool concept in String Theory, which is all about these tiny "strings" being the basic stuff of everything in the universe. So, T-Duality shows this amazing parallel between different string theories that are set up in different kinds of spacetime.

Basically, T-Duality says that if you have one String Theory all wrapped up on a tiny circle with a certain radius (let's call it R), it's actually the same as another String Theory wrapped up on a circle with a radius of 1/R. In simpler terms, what happens to a string in a small, squished space is the same as what happens in a big, stretched-out space. It's like seeing the same stuff from different angles! This idea gets really interesting when you think about how it connects theories with different numbers of dimensions or shapes. T-Duality acts like this magical bridge, linking together these different string theories.

Let's break it down with an example: Imagine you've got a String Theory on a circle with radius R. T-Duality tells us that this is just like another version of the theory on a circle with a radius of (1/R). So, what might seem tiny in one theory looks huge in the other, and vice versa. To put it into math terms, T-Duality is like this transformation: R → α' / R, where α' is this special number that's part of the string's nature. This formula basically shows how the sizes of the circles in the two theories relate to each other.

Overall, T-Duality gives us this awesome way to see String Theory, showing how things connect even when they seem totally different. It's like zooming in and out on a map and still recognizing the same landmarks. In essence, T-Duality enriches our understanding of String Theory by establishing a profound symmetry that transcends spacetime geometries, revealing unexpected connections and providing a more intricate perspective on the intricate fabric of the universe at its most fundamental level.

S-duality, also known as Strong-Weak Duality, is another mind-blowing idea in String Theory. This concept goes beyond your typical geometric transformations. It's all about linking up different string theories that have different strengths of connection between their bits and pieces, kind of like bridging the gap between theories that are either super tight or super loose.

In the world of String Theory, S-Duality uncovers this awesome symmetry that goes beyond the usual ideas of strong and weak interactions. It's like finding this hidden unity within spacetime itself. This fancy duality basically says that if you have a theory with really strong connections between its parts, it's secretly the same as a theory with really weak connections, and vice versa.

Let's break it down: Think about type IIB superString Theory. S-Duality makes this cool connection between something called the coupling constant 'g' and its opposite, '1/g'. So, when the theory is in strong coupling mode (where 'g' is big), it behaves just like it would in weak coupling mode (where 'g' is small). And when 'g' is small (meaning weak connections), the theory acts the same as when 'g' is big (meaning strong connections). Mathematically, we show this as 'g → 1/g'.

So, basically, S-Duality in String Theory is this key idea that links up theories with different strengths of connections, giving us a glimpse into how spacetime works and how the stuff in it interacts at its core

From Leaves to Branches

In essence, these dualities can be boiled down to two things: theories with different universal viewpoints are mathematically identical and theories with different levels of coupling strength have a deep connection. Using these two principles, we learn many aspects of how our universe works. Here's how it works, step-by-step:

1. We physically interact with two principles, A & B.

2. Duality says that A & B are really the same.

3. I test this out by doing an experiment with A.

4. I do the same experiment with B.

5. The results are the same

6. I do it 10,000 more times

7. The results are the same

8. A says something works over this half of the universe

9. B says something works over the other half of the universe,

10. We understand this as a single force that we call AB.

11. We understand that the AB force must work everywhere.

12. The AB principle is a universal symmetry

We name that particular symmetry and understand it as an aspect of our universe. Since we know that everything is based on the fundamental forces of the universe, we know that particular symmetry is because of the interactions of two or more fundamental forces. String Theory says those fundamental interactions come from strings.

Symmetries

Symmetry, in physics, denotes a balanced arrangement of parts where properties remain consistent post-transformation, such as rotation or reflection. In String Theory, these principles govern the universe's behavior fundamentally. The following subsections are different symmetries and aspects of symmetries.

Spacetime Symmetry

The laws of physics remain unchanged regardless of location or time, a core principle of modern physics and String Theory.

Imagine you're conducting an experiment here on Earth, and then someone else repeats the same experiment on the other side of the galaxy or even in a different era. According to the principle of space-time symmetry, both experiments should yield the same results if all other factors remain constant. This notion suggests that the laws of physics are universal and apply uniformly throughout the cosmos and across different points in time. If you drop a ball from a certain height on Earth, it will fall towards the ground due to the force of gravity. If you were to conduct the same experiment on another planet or even in the distant past or future, you would observe the same gravitational effect. This consistency is a manifestation of space-time symmetry. In the context of String Theory, space-time symmetry plays a crucial role in understanding the behavior of strings and their interactions. It implies that the fundamental laws governing the behavior of strings are invariant under transformations of space and time. This concept not only helps physicists make predictions and understand the fundamental nature of reality but also suggests that there may be underlying symmetries and principles governing the universe at its most fundamental level.

Internal Symmetry

Besides space-time symmetry, String Theory encompasses transformations impacting the internal structure of particles.

In addition to the symmetries that govern the behavior of objects in space and time, String Theory also incorporates another type of symmetry known as internal symmetry. This concept delves into the internal structure of particles, which are essentially tiny vibrating strings in String Theory. Think of internal symmetry as a sort of hidden symmetry within the particles themselves. Just as a musical string can vibrate in different patterns to produce different musical notes, the strings in String Theory can vibrate in various ways, giving rise to different particles with distinct properties such as mass, charge, and spin. Internal symmetry transformations involve changing the way these strings vibrate while keeping their overall shape and location in space-time the same.

These transformations allow us to understand how different particles are related to each other and how they transform into one another under certain conditions. By studying internal symmetries, physicists can uncover deeper insights into the underlying structure of particles and the fundamental forces that govern their interactions. This understanding is crucial for building a comprehensive theory of the universe, where both space-time symmetries and internal symmetries play integral roles in shaping the fabric of reality.

Symmetry Breaking

While apparent at high energies, symmetry breaks at lower energies, explaining distinct forces despite potential unification at higher energies.

In String Theory, the concept of symmetry breaking refers to a phenomenon where the symmetries present at high energies appear to break down or become hidden at lower energies. This means that although different forces may seem unified at very high energies, they appear distinct and separate at lower energies. Imagine a scenario where all the fundamental forces of nature, such as gravity, electromagnetism, the weak nuclear force, and the strong nuclear force, were once unified into a single, symmetrical framework at extremely high energies, like those present in the early universe. However, as the universe cooled and energy levels decreased, this symmetrical state was disrupted, causing the forces to manifest in distinct ways.

Symmetry breaking in String Theory provides a mechanism for explaining why we observe separate forces in our everyday experiences, even though they may have originated from a single unified force at higher energies. This phenomenon helps reconcile the differences between the forces we observe, such as gravity and the other fundamental forces, while still allowing for the possibility of their unification at higher energies. By understanding how symmetries break at lower energies, string theorists can gain insights into the nature of the universe at both high and low energy scales. This concept is crucial for developing a comprehensive understanding of the fundamental forces and their interactions in the cosmos.

Conformal Symmetry

This one is much more complicated.

String Theory maintains invariance under conformal transformations, crucial for consistent physical calculations across frames of reference.

In String Theory, conformal symmetry is a fundamental concept that plays a crucial role in maintaining consistency across different frames of reference. Essentially, it refers to the idea that the theory remains unchanged under certain transformations that alter the scale but preserve the angles and shapes of objects. This means that even if you stretch or shrink space and time in a particular way, the underlying laws of physics described by String Theory remain the same.

Conformal transformations are particularly important because they allow physicists to perform calculations and make predictions that are independent of the specific scale or size of the system being studied. This is incredibly useful because it means that the theory can accurately describe phenomena at both microscopic and macroscopic scales without needing to adjust parameters for each scale separately. For example, imagine you're studying the behavior of strings in a particular spacetime background. Conformal symmetry ensures that your calculations will give the same results regardless of whether you're considering a tiny portion of space or the entire universe, as long as the underlying conformal symmetry is preserved. This property of String Theory is essential for maintaining its mathematical consistency and predictive power, making it a powerful framework for exploring the fundamental nature of the universe across different scales and frames of reference.

Supersymmetry

The theory exhibits symmetry between bosonic and fermionic states, essential for stability and avoiding quantum calculation issues.

In String Theory, an intriguing concept known as supersymmetry plays a crucial role in maintaining stability and resolving certain quantum calculation challenges. Essentially, supersymmetry introduces a symmetry between two fundamental types of particles: bosons and fermions. Bosons are particles that carry forces, like photons and gluons, while fermions are the building blocks of matter, such as electrons and quarks. By establishing a symmetry between bosonic and fermionic states, supersymmetry helps to balance the forces and matter components within the theory. This balance is essential for stability, preventing the theory from becoming mathematically inconsistent or unstable.

Supersymmetry plays a key role in avoiding certain quantum calculation issues that can arise in theories without this symmetry. In essence, supersymmetry provides a framework that allows for a more elegant and unified description of the fundamental particles and forces in the universe. It is a crucial aspect of String Theory that has sparked much interest and exploration in the quest to understand the underlying nature of reality.

—

Scattering Amplitude

In String Theory, we look at how tiny strings interact in space. We use fancy math tools like worldsheet Conformal Field Theory and Riemann surface integrals to understand these interactions, like unraveling a bunch of tangled wires. These interactions are shown through something called Feynman diagrams, which help us understand how strings scatter when they collide. These scattering amplitudes basically tell us the chances of strings bouncing off each other after a crash. It's like predicting what happens when two cars collide. Studying these amplitudes helps us learn more about how these tiny strings work together.

Riemann's Surface Integral

String Theory relies on sophisticated mathematical tools to study these interactions. Worldsheet conformal field theory deals with the dynamics of strings propagating through spacetime, while Riemann surface integrals help us figure out the likelihood of different collisions between strings.

Here's a more detailed explanation:

A Riemann surface is a mathematical object that helps us understand complex relationships between points in space. In String Theory, we can use Riemann surfaces to describe the paths that strings take as they move through space and time. These surfaces provide a way to calculate the probabilities or likelihoods of different types of string interactions. Think of it like this: if you're trying to predict the likelihood of different outcomes when you roll a pair of dice, you might use a mathematical formula to figure out the chances of rolling a specific number. In the same way, physicists use Riemann surface integrals to calculate the chances of different types of string collisions happening. When someone (most likely a physicist) says, "Riemann surface integrals help us figure out the likelihood of different collisions between strings", in the context of String Theory, they're basically saying that this mathematical tool helps us understand how strings interact with each other and what kinds of outcomes we can expect from those interactions. It's like having a special calculator that helps us unravel the mysteries of the universe at its most fundamental level.

Feynman's Diagrams

Imagine you're trying to understand how particles interact with each other, like electrons bouncing off each other or emitting photons. It's like watching a complex dance where particles exchange energy and momentum. Feynman diagrams are like choreography for this dance—they're visual representations that help physicists understand and calculate these interactions. (It also helps to note that Feynman diagrams obey conservation laws, like the conservation of energy and momentum, meaning that the total energy and momentum going into an interaction must equal the total energy and momentum coming out of it).

Each line represents a particle. A straight line might represent an electron, a wavy line might represent a photon, and so on. These lines show the paths that particles take as they interact. Where lines meet in the diagram, it represents a moment of interaction between particles. These interaction points are called vertices. For example, if an electron emits a photon, you'd see a vertex where the electron line and the photon line meet. The direction of the lines in the diagram matters. For example, an arrow might indicate the direction of particle flow or the direction of time.

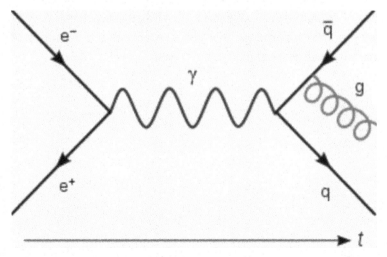

In this Feynman diagram, an electron (e–) and a positron (e+) annihilate, producing a photon (γ, represented by the blue sine wave) that becomes a quark–antiquark pair (quark q, antiquark q̄), after which the antiquark radiates a gluon (g, represented by the green helix). This is all over the movement of time (t).

Now, why are Feynman diagrams so useful?

They provide a visual way to represent complex particle interactions. Instead of dealing with long and complicated equations, physicists can look at a Feynman diagram and quickly understand what's happening in a particle interaction. These diagrams also help physicists calculate the probability amplitudes for different particle interactions. By assigning mathematical expressions to each part of the diagram, physicists can perform calculations to predict the likelihood of certain outcomes in particle collisions or decays. They can be applied across different theories of particle physics, from quantum electrodynamics to the standard model of particle physics, making them a powerful tool for understanding a wide range of physical phenomena.

String Theory employs Feynman diagrams to visualize and calculate scattering amplitudes. However, in String Theory, these diagrams represent interactions between strings rather than point particles. Understanding these diagrams helps us comprehend the dynamics of string scattering.

The following paragraph is an excerpt from the American Butterfly series, The Network on a String, in which the author, Nick Ray Ball, attempts to use analogies to explain String Theory in an understandable way. In this chapter, Ball uses Feynman Diagrams to compare the understanding of particle theory to String Theory. Ball uses essentially the same as the previous diagram when explaining particle theory. This is Ball's Feynman Diagram for String Theory.

Feynman Diagram for Strings

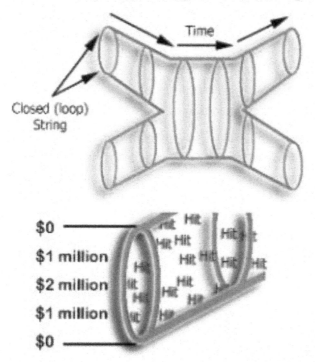

"*If we look at the Feynman Diagram… we see how this works within physics. We see the version where all probabilities fall within the loop of a string, and all can be accounted for. If we look at the bottom section of the diagram… [instead of] a point particle or individual network, which needs to generate a fixed figure… the range for success is far more flexible as the network is now effectively built out of strings. The strings of networks work as one. Looking always to balance and protect the weakest individual parts of the network" (Ball).*

The Particles' Private Information

The scattering amplitudes contain a wealth of information about the underlying String Theory, including details about the particles involved, their energies, and the nature of their interactions. Analyzing these amplitudes provides valuable insights into the theory and its predictions. In the context of scattering amplitudes, the "particles" involved refer to vibrational modes of the fundamental strings. Nevertheless, the term "particle" is used in conventional Quantum Field Theory. In the context of String Theory, there are two types of particles/string-vibrations: Open and Closed.

Open Strings

Visualize a flexible strand, resembling a jump rope, extending infinitely in both directions. Within the realm of String Theory, this object represents what is known as an "open string." These strings possess the remarkable ability to oscillate and vibrate in various patterns and modes, akin to the strings of a musical instrument such as a guitar. However, what distinguishes open strings in the context of String Theory is their connection to specialized surfaces known as D-branes. These D-branes serve as anchor points or endpoints for the open strings, providing them with a tangible boundary to interact with. It is on these D-branes that the open strings find purchase, allowing them to adhere and oscillate in distinct ways. The manner in which these open strings vibrate and oscillate yields valuable insights into the nature of fundamental particles. Each unique vibrational pattern corresponds to a specific particle state. For instance, when an open string vibrates in a particular mode, it may exhibit characteristics analogous to those of an electron, while a different vibrational pattern could manifest qualities reminiscent of a quark.

In essence, the study of open strings within String Theory revolves around deciphering the intricate relationships between the vibrational modes of these strings and the properties of fundamental particles. While conventional quantum field theory offers one avenue for exploration, String Theory emerges as the most compelling and sophisticated framework for understanding these phenomena in contemporary physics.

These are some particles in conventional Quantum Field Theory that correspond to vibrations in open strings:

Electrons = Excitations of open strings attached to D-branes. Electrons are fundamental particles with a negative charge.

Neutrinos = Minor excitations of open strings. These are neutral, weakly-interacting particles.

Quarks = Open strings themselves. Quarks can be combined to form hadrons (protons and neutrons)

Gauge Bosons = Specific vibrational modes of open strings. These correspond to three of the four fundamental forces of the universe: photons (for electromagnetism), gluons (for the strong force), W & Z bosons (for the weak force). String Theory posits that the fourth fundamental force, gravity, is actually a result of the vibrations of closed strings.

Muons, Tau Particles, & Their Neutrinos = Different vibrational modes of open strings. These are other matter particles predicted by particle physics.

Closed Strings

Consider a string that forms a closed loop by connecting with itself, resembling the structure of a rubber band. Within the framework of String Theory, this configuration is referred to as a "closed string." Similar to their open counterparts, closed strings possess the remarkable capacity to oscillate and vibrate in various modes and patterns. However, unlike open strings, which have distinct endpoints, closed strings lack such terminations due to their closed loop structure. Consequently, closed strings do not possess free ends, but rather form continuous loops. Despite this difference, the vibrational modes of closed strings remain a crucial aspect of their behavior within String Theory. Just as with open strings, the diverse vibrational patterns exhibited by closed strings encode valuable information about the nature and properties of fundamental particles.

In essence, the study of closed strings in String Theory involves elucidating the intricate relationship between the vibrational modes of these closed loops and the characteristics of different particles. Through analyzing these vibrational patterns, physicists gain insights into the fundamental building blocks of the universe and the underlying structure of spacetime.

These are some types of particles and how they match with closed strings:

Graviton = The lowest vibrational mode of closed strings. It's a massless particle that mediates the gravitational force.

Photon = Excitations of closed strings in certain modes.

Gluon = Excitations of closed strings in other modes. These particles mediate the strong force, binding quarks together in hadrons.

Scalar Bosons = Certain vibrational modes of closed strings. These are hypothetical particles with spin 0.

Gravitinos: Specific patterns of vibrations that closed strings can undergo in certain types of string theories. These vibrations correspond to different modes of oscillation of the strings. In supersymmetric string theories, some of these vibrational modes correspond to the creation of particles known as gravitinos. Gravitinos are the supersymmetric partners of the graviton, which is the particle associated with the gravitational force. So, when closed strings vibrate in these specific ways, they give rise to gravitinos, which are essential for understanding certain aspects of gravity within the framework of supersymmetric string theories.

Seeing It In-Person

Just having an idea isn't enough. Scientists need to check if the theories actually match up with what we see in the real world.

They make predictions using math based on String Theory. These predictions tell them what they should see if String Theory is right. Then, they go and look at what happens in real experiments. If what they see matches their predictions, it demonstrates that the math may be correct.

To make these predictions, they use something called "scattering amplitudes." Think of scattering as when you throw a ball against a wall and it bounces off. Amplitudes are like a score that tells you how likely it is for the ball to bounce in a certain way. In String Theory, these amplitudes help scientists connect the math they do with what they see in experiments. So, when they compare their predicted amplitudes with what they actually measure in experiments, it's like checking their work. If they match up, it's a big win! It means String Theory might be a really good way to understand the basic rules of how everything in the universe works. But if they don't match, it's back to the drawing board, trying to figure out what went wrong and maybe tweaking their theory to make it fit better with what we see in the real world. These scattering amplitudes in String Theory serve as a powerful tool for exploring the fundamental interactions of strings and understanding the underlying structure of spacetime at a microscopic level. They rely on advanced mathematical techniques and provide a means to bridge theoretical predictions with experimental data, ultimately advancing our understanding of the universe.

—

C F T

In this section, we embark on a journey to unravel the intricate mathematical underpinnings that form the backbone of String Theory. Don't worry if these terms sound intimidating at first; I'm here to break them down into digestible pieces.

Conformal field theory (CFT) is like the blueprint guiding our understanding of String Theory, a theory that proposes that the fundamental building blocks of the universe are not particles but tiny, vibrating strings. These strings dance through spacetime, creating the rich tapestry of our reality. But to truly comprehend their behavior, we need the tools of mathematics, and that's where CFT steps in.

At the heart of CFT lies the concept of conformal symmetry. Imagine you have a piece of rubber representing spacetime, and you can stretch, squeeze, and warp it without tearing. Conformal symmetry tells us that certain transformations – like these deformations – leave the underlying physics unchanged. This profound symmetry unlocks a treasure trove of insights into the behavior of strings and their interactions.

One of the key ideas in CFT is how things change as we zoom in or out – a concept known as scale invariance. Think of zooming in on a fractal: no matter how much you magnify it, the same patterns emerge. We'll explore how properties of systems remain unchanged under certain scale transformations, shedding light on the behavior of strings at different length scales. In CFT, we not only study individual strings but also how they interact and influence each other. Through tools like correlation functions, we peek into the intricate dance of strings, understanding how they correlate and influence one another across spacetime. These visual interactions paint a vivid picture of the underlying dynamics at play. CFT also reveals a remarkable unity in seemingly disparate systems. Just as different musical notes harmonize to create a symphony, CFT shows us how seemingly unrelated phenomena in physics can be different manifestations of the same underlying principles. It's like discovering that the same melody echoes through different instruments. Lastly, we'll bridge the gap between CFT and String Theory, showcasing how these two fields intertwine. Through this connection, we unlock profound insights into the nature of spacetime, quantum mechanics, and gravity – laying the groundwork for a deeper understanding of the universe.

In this chapter, we'll delve into the mathematical machinery of CFT, demystifying its complexities and revealing the beauty of its concepts. So, buckle up, as we embark on a thrilling adventure through the world of conformal field theory – where mathematical elegance meets the fundamental fabric of reality.

We can understand CFT through three major ideas that break down into seven total steps.

Idea 1: CFT allows for conformal symmetry.

To understand conformal symmetry, we must first understand the context of math in the subatomic world, then we need to understand CFT, then we can finally understand conformal symmetry.

Quantum Field Theory

Imagine you have a big field, like a soccer field, but instead of grass, it's filled with tiny, invisible particles popping in and out of existence all the time. These particles are like the players on the soccer field, constantly moving around and interacting with each other. Now, in quantum field theory (QFT), we study how these particles and their interactions work on this field. In the quantum world, things can be a bit more unpredictable and weirder. One of the key ideas in quantum field theory is that particles aren't just little balls bouncing around. Instead, they're excitations or vibrations in their respective fields. It's like if you pluck a guitar string and it creates a sound wave traveling through the air. Similarly, when something happens in the field, like two particles interacting, it creates ripples or waves that we can think of as particles.

When dealing with the subatomic world, we can't predict with certainty where a particle will be or what it will do. This is called quantum uncertainty. Instead, we use probabilities to describe its behavior. It's like trying to guess where a soccer player will move next on the field – you can't know for sure, but you can make educated guesses based on probabilities.

Some particles act as messengers for other particles. Imagine two players kicking a soccer ball back and forth. In the quantum world, this is represented by the exchange of particles called "force carriers," like photons for electromagnetic force or gluons for the strong nuclear force. These particles mediate the interaction between other particles, just like the ball mediates the interaction between the players.

Overall, quantum field theory is a way for scientists to understand the fundamental building blocks of the universe.

Conformal Field Theory

Conformal field theory (CFT) is a special version of QFT where the symmetry of the theory prevents any changes to the angles between the fields.

Imagine you have a bunch of objects scattered across a field, and you're not allowed to rotate them or change the angles between them. This restriction makes things simpler because you don't have to worry about how the objects are oriented relative to each other – they always maintain the same angles. In CFT, these "objects" are actually fields, representing different particles or interactions in the theory. The conformal symmetry basically says that no matter how you stretch, squeeze, or deform the field, the angles between the fields remain unchanged.

This might sound a bit abstract, but it has some powerful implications. For one, it simplifies the mathematical description of the theory. Without conformal symmetry, you'd have to consider all sorts of complicated transformations that could change the angles between the fields, making the math much harder. But with conformal symmetry in place, you can focus on the essential aspects of the theory without getting bogged down in unnecessary details.

In essence, conformal field theory is a special kind of quantum field theory that benefits from this symmetry, making it more manageable and easier to study. It's like having a set of rules that simplify the game, allowing scientists to delve deeper into the fundamental properties of the universe.

Conformal Symmetry

Conformal symmetry is a special type of symmetry that preserves angles between points.

Mathematically, we can represent this as follows: Suppose we have a transformation T that acts on points x in our space. Conformal symmetry requires that if we have three points, x1, x2, x3, forming an angle θ before the transformation, then after the transformation, the angle between the transformed points remains the same.

$$\angle(\, x1,\, x2,\, x3\,) = \angle (\, T(\, x1\,),\, T(\, x2\,),\, T(\, x3\,)\,).$$

This property ensures that the fundamental geometry of the space is preserved under conformal transformations. In terms of mathematical equations, conformal transformations are often expressed using complex numbers and transformations like scaling, translation, rotation, and inversion. The most general conformal transformation in two dimensions can be written as:

$$z' = \frac{az+b}{cz+d}$$

The usefulness of this step lies in providing a precise mathematical framework for describing conformal transformations. It allows us to apply mathematical tools from complex analysis to analyze and understand conformal symmetry.

Now, let's count to three.

One: Conformal transformations are certain types of coordinate transformations that preserve angles but not necessarily distances. The thing behaves the same way regardless of how you stretch, compress, or distort the space or time coordinates.

Two: Conformal invariance is the attribute of a physical theory where equations are the same even under conformal transformations.

Three: Conformal symmetry plays a crucial role in shaping the behavior of correlation functions within a theory that adheres to conformal invariance. These correlation functions essentially depict the relationships and behaviors of various fields within the theory across different points in space and time. Leveraging conformal symmetry often allows us to streamline the computation of these correlation functions and glean significant insights into the underlying physics of the system.

The mathematical framework of conformal symmetry serves as a robust tool for analyzing and comprehending conformal field theories. By imposing constraints on how fields transform under conformal transformations, we simplify the mathematical depiction of the theory and uncover essential insights into its core properties.

Idea 2: The processes that underpin String Theory.

These three major concepts are the mathematical basis for String Theory: things are different at scale, mathematical operators must expand, and different parts of this mathematical system are part of one cohesive identity.

Difference At Scale

Renormalization Group Flow: This refers to how physical quantities change as you zoom in or out on different length scales. For example, imagine you're looking at a group of trees in a forest. If you zoom in, you might see individual leaves and branches. But if you zoom out, you see the forest as a whole. The Renormalization Group Flow helps us understand how the properties of the trees, like their density or height, change as we zoom in or out.

In the context of String Theory, CFT helps us understand how properties of String Theory evolve as we change the scale at which we observe them. We describe the vibrations of strings using mathematical equations. These equations tell us how the string moves and vibrates through space and time. Now, when we zoom in or out on the string, we're essentially changing the scale at which we're observing its vibrations.

Mathematically, let's say we have a function that describes the vibration of the string. We can represent this function as $\Psi(x, t)$, where x represents the positing along the string, and t represents time.

This function gives us information about how the string vibrates at each point along its length and at each moment in time. When we use CFT to understand these vibrations at different scales, we're essentially studying how this function changes as we change the scale of observation. We can represent this change in scale using a mathematical parameter, let's call it λ. When λ is small, we're zooming in on the string, and when λ is large, we're zooming out.

For example, let's say we have an equation that describes the energy of the string vibrations:

$$E = f(\lambda) \, \Psi(x,t).$$

Here, $f(\lambda)$ represents a mathematical function that depends on λ. By using techniques from Conformal Field Theory, we can study how $f(\lambda)$ changes as we vary λ, and how this, in turn, affects the energy of the string vibrations.

By analyzing these transformations, we can uncover patterns and relationships that help us better understand the nature of String Theory. It's like adjusting the focus on a microscope to see how the details of the string's vibrations change as we look at them on different scales. And with the help of Conformal Field Theory, we can explore these changes mathematically, gaining deeper insights into the behavior of strings in the universe.

Operator Expansions

In CFT, operator product expansions (OPEs) describe how operators (which represent physical observables) combine and interact with each other. Understanding these expansions is crucial for analyzing the behavior of strings and their interactions. In Conformal Field Theory, we often use mathematical objects called operators to represent physical observables. These operators could be things like energy, momentum, or other properties of the system we're studying. Think of them like tools we use to measure different aspects of the system. Now, Operator Product Expansions (OPEs) describe how these operators combine and interact with each other. It's like understanding how different tools work together to give us information about the system we're studying.

Mathematically, let's say we have two operators, $A(z)$ and $B(w)$, where z and w are complex numbers representing points in space and time. The OPE tells us how the product of these two operators,

A(z) × B(w), can be expanded into a sum of terms involving other operators and some coefficients.

$$A(z) \times B(w) = \sum_i C_i(z - w)^{h_i - h_A - h_B} \mathcal{O}_i(w)$$

Now, let's unpack this a bit. The OPE tells us that when we multiply the operators **A(z)** and **B(w)** together at different points **z** and **w**, we get a sum of terms involving other operators **Oi** at point **w**. Each term in the sum tells us how these operators interact with each other and how they contribute to the overall behavior of the system.

Understanding these expansions is crucial for analyzing the behavior of strings and their interactions in Conformal Field Theory. It's like having a toolkit that allows us to dissect the system into its fundamental components and understand how they work together to create the behavior we observe. By studying these OPEs, we can gain insights into the underlying structure of the theory and uncover important relationships between different observables. It's like solving a puzzle where each piece (operator) contributes to the overall picture, helping us understand the behavior of strings and their interactions in the universe.

Different Parts, Same System

Correlation functions in CFT describe how different parts of a system are related to each other. In String Theory, CFT helps us understand the relationships between different aspects of string behavior and their effects on observable quantities.

In everyday life and in many branches of physics, we often want to understand how different parts of a system are related to each other. Mathematically, correlation functions are tools we use to measure these relationships. They tell us how the behavior of one part of the system is correlated or connected to the behavior of another part.

In the context of String Theory, these correlation functions help us uncover relationships between various properties of strings, like their vibrations, interactions, and other characteristics. Imagine you have a group of friends who like to play musical instruments. You might notice that when one friend starts playing a melody on the guitar, another friend might start tapping their foot to the beat. This is a correlation between the music being played and the foot-tapping – when one changes, the other tends to change too. In String Theory, correlation functions help us identify similar connections between different aspects of string behavior.

Idea 3: Conformal symmetry works with String Theory.

The profound connection between CFT and String Theory means that many properties of String Theory can be understood and derived using the tools and concepts of CFT. This connection is what allows String Theory to exhibit unique and remarkable properties that distinguish it from conventional quantum field theories.

In short, conformal field theory provides the mathematical framework necessary for understanding the behavior of strings in String Theory. It allows us to analyze how strings move and interact, describe their properties, and derive important results that distinguish String Theory from other theories in physics.

–

Quantization

Before you play chess, you must first understand how the pieces move.

Quantizing strings in String Theory helps us understand the basic ingredients of the universe and how they "dance" together to create everything we see around us. Quantization the process of breaking a big problem into smaller, manageable pieces. As seen in the previous section, string movement is incredibly complex, so we break down how the string twists and wiggles in different ways. Since we understand that the string's movement creates particles, by chopping up the string's movement into understandable parts, we can figure out what specific particles are created and how they interact with each other. Some vibrations represent particles that are really light and move super-fast, like particles of light called photons or the force-carrying particles of the strong and weak nuclear forces. These are called massless particles. Other vibrations correspond to particles that have some heft to them, like electrons or quarks. These particles have mass and move a bit slower. And then there are some vibrations that are a bit strange – they correspond to particles that have a negative mass squared, which might sound like a contradiction, but in the world of quantum mechanics, things can get a bit weird like that - in that they don't match our visual, classical understanding and intuition.

Quantizing strings in String Theory is like studying the tiny, vibrating strings of the universe to unlock the secrets of how everything fits together. It's a bit like solving a giant puzzle, where each piece – each vibration of the string – gives us a clue about the bigger picture of the cosmos. And by putting all those clues together, we can gain a deeper understanding of the universe and how it came to be.

I divided this chapter into four separate parts to better understand string movement: the rules, the moving, the math, and everything.

Part 1 is about describing the string as a quantum object, so it follows the quantum world's rules. **Part 2** describes the particle types that correspond to string vibrations. **Part 3** describes the type of math we have to do with these strings. **Part 4** describes what it means for strings to interact.

These parts lead to a cohesive understanding of the fundamentals of string movement in small sections.

Part 1: Quantizing Quanta

In String Theory, quantization involves treating the string as a minuscule vibrating entity governed by quantum mechanics rather than classical physics. Rather than envisioning the string's movement as smooth and continuous, we analyze it in terms of discrete units. In the mathematical framework of String Theory, we utilize a concept known as a path integral to comprehend the transitions between different shapes that the string can undergo. To illustrate, imagine determining all possible routes from your home to the store. A path integral aggregates the probabilities associated with each conceivable path, much like summing up the likelihood of each possible journey. Therefore, when computing a path integral for a string, we're essentially summing up the probabilities of it traversing all feasible paths between its various shapes.

In the context of String Theory, "normal modes" denote the diverse patterns in which a string can vibrate or oscillate. Analogous to plucking a guitar string which produces different tones through various vibrational patterns, a string in String Theory can vibrate in multiple patterns, each corresponding to a distinct "normal mode". These normal modes encapsulate the fundamental vibrational characteristics of the string, offering insights into its motion and behavior. Mathematically, we express the string's coordinates through a series that encompasses terms for each of these normal modes. Additionally, we employ operators to symbolize the creation and annihilation of these modes.

Part 2: Types of Particles

When we delve into the concept of quantizing the string within String Theory, we're delving into the microscopic realm, examining how the string behaves on the smallest possible scale. Imagine the string as if it's composed of minuscule strings vibrating in various ways. Now, these vibrations, they're not just random movements; each movement corresponds to a specific type of particle.

Massless States

First off, let's talk about the lightweights of the particle world - the massless states. Picture these particles as weightless travelers, zooming around the cosmos without any baggage of mass to slow them down. Examples of such ethereal particles include the graviton, a theoretical particle believed to carry the gravitational force, and gauge bosons, which are like messengers of fundamental forces such as electromagnetism. These particles arise from string vibrations that possess zero mass.

Massive States

On the flip side, we've got the heavyweights - the massive states. These particles carry some weight and move through space in a distinct manner. Think of fermions, the tiny building blocks of matter like electrons and quarks, and massive bosons, which are responsible for forces like the weak nuclear force, exemplified by the W and Z bosons. These particles emerge from string vibrations that possess nonzero mass.

Tachyonic States

Now, here's where it gets intriguing. There exist vibrations representing what we call tachyonic states. These vibrations have a quirky characteristic: initially, they appear to possess a negative squared mass, which might sound baffling. Initially, this oddity posed a challenge because it didn't align with our observations of the universe. However, in specific scenarios or contexts within String Theory, these tachyonic states find interpretations that fit logically. Remember, String Theory is inherently mathematical, and the pure logic of math sometimes supersedes our intuitive understanding, but when intuition fails, trust is necessary for understanding. In our case, our intuitive sense of things having mass fails when it comes to the subatomic world, so we must trust that since the math works out, it must be logical. According to String Theory, things can have some mass, no mass, or negative mass, but despite their peculiar nature at first glance, they play a vital role in the theory, aiding our comprehension of string behavior under particular circumstances.

Part 3: Commutation Relations

In the realm of String Theory, commutation relations are like discovering a secret code that unlocks the mysteries of the quantum world. Let's break it down:

Imagine trying to understand a messy room. Commutation relations are like rules that help us tidy up and find patterns in the mess. They reveal the hidden order in the chaos of quantum mechanics, helping us make sense of how things work at the tiniest scales. Think of quantization as putting together a puzzle. Commutation relations are like the pieces that fit together to make the picture clear. They tell us how different aspects of quantum systems relate to each other, helping us solve the puzzle of how the universe operates on a fundamental level. Understanding these rules is key to mastering the game of quantum physics; discovering hidden connections between things you never thought were related. Commutation relations show us how different properties of particles, like their position and momentum, are connected in strange and surprising ways. It's like finding out that your favorite song and your math homework are somehow linked! Studying commutation relations helps us put all the pieces together to see the big picture of how the universe works.

The strings in String Theory don't have political opinions, but they are either "pro" or "anti" commute. Since commutation relations are the mathematical rules of strings when we treat them like quantum objects, being "pro" or "anti" commutation is simply the nature in which these strings behave. A string is inherently either pro-commutation or anti-commutation in the same way that we use pi = 3.14 when we do simple math, but we use pi = 3.14159265... for high-level geometry. We're using pi for both types of analyses, but one requires more specific information. We only need simple algebra for bosonic strings, but superstrings require a higher, more specific mathematical framework for it to work.

Pro Commutation Relations

This is about how operations behave when they're done in different orders. Imagine you're doing a simple math problem, like multiplying two numbers. Now, think about a special kind of string called a "bosonic string." These strings are like the basic building blocks of the universe, but they're simpler compared to some other types. When we talk about bosonic strings and how they behave in math, we use something called "canonical commutation relations." It's like having a rulebook for how these strings interact. With bosonic strings, if you swap the order of two steps, something surprising happens – the final result changes its sign. If you were multiplying two numbers and you decided to switch the order in which you multiplied them, you'd usually get the same answer. But with bosonic strings, swapping the order of certain operations can make the result positive or negative, kind of like flipping a coin.

Anti-Commutation Relations

Now, let's switch gears slightly. Instead of changing the sign when we swap the order of two operators, anti-commutation relations keep the sign but add a minus sign. You're still doing math, but now you're dealing with more complex strings called "superstrings." These superstrings are the next level up from bosonic strings and include something called "fermionic degrees of freedom," which basically means they have some extra properties compared to simpler strings. Now, when we talk about how these superstrings behave in math, we introduce something called "anti-commutation relations." These relations keep the sign of the operation but add a minus sign when you swap the order of certain steps. Mathematically, we represent this with something called an "anti-commutator," which looks like this: **{A, B}**. When we calculate the anti-commutator of two operations **A** and **B**, we use the formula **AB + BA**. This formula ensures that when we swap the order of **A** and **B**, we get a negative result added to the original result.

So, when we're working with strings in the context of String Theory, it's incredibly important to make sure that our operations follow either commutation or anti-commutation relations. This ensures that we're accurately treating strings as quantum objects and that our calculations truly reflect how they behave at the quantum level. It's like following the right set of rules to make sure our math matches up with the real-world behavior of these superstrings.

Part 4: Dynamics

Interactions among strings in String Theory are pivotal to understanding their behavior and the dynamics that govern their movement through spacetime. Much like particles in particle physics experiments, strings can collide, merge, or scatter off each other, revealing insights into their fundamental nature and the structure of spacetime.

When strings interact, they provide a window into the underlying mechanisms that shape the behavior of matter and energy at the most fundamental level. By studying these interactions, physicists can uncover the microscopic intricacies of the universe and gain a deeper understanding of the fundamental laws of nature. String scattering, in particular, plays a crucial role in shaping the behavior of strings. As strings collide or scatter off each other, they undergo complex processes that lead to a variety of outcomes. These interactions are akin to the interactions observed between particles, but with the added complexity of string dynamics.

Worldsheet interactions, which describe how strings move and interact within their two-dimensional worldsheet, further contribute to the rich phenomena observed in String Theory. These interactions dictate how strings evolve over time and how they influence each other's trajectories through spacetime. The role of interaction vertices is also significant. These vertices represent the points where strings come into contact and exchange energy, momentum, and other properties. Understanding the dynamics of these interaction vertices is crucial for modeling string interactions accurately and predicting their outcomes.

Overall, interactions among strings shape the rich and diverse phenomena observed in String Theory. By treating strings as fundamental quantum objects and quantizing their behavior, String Theory provides a unified framework for understanding the fundamental constituents of nature and the intricate web of interactions that govern their behavior.

Stringematics

Stringematics is a term unique to this book and created by fusing String Theory and Kinematics (the physical study of motion). This section is essentially a deep dive into the String Equations of Motion. In this section, we embark on a profound exploration of the string equations of motion, unraveling the intricacies that underpin the very essence of reality.

In this section, we delve into the core concepts of string theory, breaking them down into easily digestible chapters:

We begin by unraveling the Nambu-Goto action, which describes how strings move through spacetime by considering the area they sweep out. Through simple explanations and relatable examples, we uncover the dynamics of relativistic strings and their behavior in the cosmic dance of the universe.

Building upon our understanding of string dynamics, we introduce the Polyakov action, a crucial extension that enhances our ability to describe string behavior. We explore how the Polyakov action introduces flexibility in describing string dynamics and how it incorporates the concept of reparameterization invariance.

Next, we delve into the Euler-Lagrange equations, powerful tools derived from the principle of least action. These equations provide a systematic framework for finding the equations of motion for strings in string theory. With clear explanations and illustrative examples, we unlock the secrets of how strings evolve over time.

Finally, we piece together all that we've learned to unveil the equation of motion for strings. This equation, derived from the Euler-Lagrange equations and the chosen action, serves as the cornerstone of string theory. Through its mathematical elegance and profound implications, we gain insight into how strings move through spacetime and govern the fabric of reality.

Join us as we embark on a voyage of discovery through the captivating realm of Stringematics, where the mysteries of the universe are illuminated by the delicate dance of vibrating strings. This section, as well as other sections in String Theory, are based on mathematical equations. I've done my best to explain how and why each part of the math works, including explaining the fundamentals conceptually. If all goes well in the production of this work, an individual who is not familiar with calculus but does understand a high-school level of algebra should be able to follow along with the math. Everything complicated is simple if you're patient enough to understand the nuance.

Nambu-Goto Action

The Nambu-Goto action explains how strings move in space and time by looking at the area they cover. It helps us understand how the strings bend and stretch as they move. This provides a straightforward approach to describe string dynamics and is particularly useful for understanding the classical behavior of strings.

Terms & Conditions of the Nambu-Goto Action:

Action (S): In physics, the action is a functional that quantifies the dynamics of a system. For the Nambu-Goto action, it is given by the integral of the square root of the determinant of the induced metric on the string's worldsheet.

Worldsheet (σ): The worldsheet is a two-dimensional surface swept out by the string as it moves through spacetime. It is parametrized by coordinates (σ^0, σ^1), where σ^0 and σ^1 are often referred to as "time" and "space" coordinates on the worldsheet. Essentially, it's a mathematical stand in for spacetime.

Induced Metric (y_ab): This metric describes the geometry of the worldsheet as embedded in the spacetime manifold. It is derived from the spacetime metric and serves to measure distances and angles on the worldsheet.

Determinant (det): In linear algebra, the determinant of a matrix provides information about its properties. In the context of the Nambu-Goto action, the determinant of the induced metric is essential for calculating the action.

String Tension (T): This measures how much the string resists stretching.

Integral over the worldsheet ($\int d^2\sigma$): This represents the entire area swept out by the string.

Metric Tensor on the worldsheet (Y_ab): It describes the distances between points on the surface of the worldsheet.

The Full Equation

$$S = -T \int d^2\sigma \sqrt{-\gamma}$$

In mathematical transliteration, it's this:

THIS ACTION IS EXACTLY THE NEGATIVE STRING TENSION MULTIPLIED BY THE INTEGRATION OF THE INTEGRAL OVER THE WORLDSHEET AND THE SQUARE ROOT OF THE REAL DETERMINANT OF THE METRIC TENSOR ON THE WORLDSHEET.

The negative inside the square root indicates that the metric tensor on the worldsheet is a real value and well-defined.

In plain English, it's this:

THE NAMBU GOTO ACTION IS NEGATIVELY AFFECTED BY THE STRING'S TENSION, BUT THE ENTIRE AREA SWEPT OUT BY THE STRING IS INTEGRATED WITH THE REAL DISTANCES BETWEEN POINTS.

If the distances between points on the worldsheet change without the string stretching, then the worldsheet is bending and/or stretching.

Polyakov Action

The Polyakov action builds on the Nambu-Goto action by adding a new way to measure the space where strings move. This helps describe string movement better, ensuring that how they move doesn't change based on how we choose to measure their space. The Polyakov action is particularly useful for quantizing strings and studying their quantum behavior. It simplifies the mathematical formalism compared to the Nambu-Goto action.

Terms & Conditions of the Polyakov Action:

Action (S): In physics, the action is a functional that quantifies the dynamics of a system. For the Nambu-Goto action, it is given by the integral of the square root of the determinant of the induced metric on the string's worldsheet.

Worldsheet (σ): The worldsheet is a two-dimensional surface swept out by the string as it moves through spacetime. It is parametrized by coordinates (σ^0, σ^1), where σ^0 and σ^1 are often referred to as "time" and "space" coordinates on the worldsheet. Essentially, it's a mathematical stand in for spacetime.

String Tension (T): This measures how much the string resists stretching.

Integral over the worldsheet ($\int d^2\sigma$): This represents the entire area swept out by the string.

Worldsheet Metric (h_ab): This metric is introduced in the Polyakov action and represents the intrinsic geometry of the worldsheet. It is used to measure distances and angles on the worldsheet independently of its embedding in spacetime.

The Polyakov Action (S _Polyakov): This quantifies the dynamics of the string.

Worldsheet Element (d^2σ): An infinitesimal area.

Inverse Worldsheet Metric (h^[ab]): This is used to raise indices in the expression.

The Volume Element: The square root of negative "h": This takes into account how the worldsheet stretches or shrinks due to the presence of the string.

Reparametrization Invariance: This is a symmetry property of the Polyakov action, meaning that the dynamics of the string remain unchanged under arbitrary reparametrizations of the worldsheet coordinates. It leads to constraints on the equations of motion and simplifies the quantization procedure.

$$h^{ab} \partial_a X^\mu \partial_b X_\mu$$: This represents the kinetic energy of the string. The two letters that look like inverse sixes are each a mathematical term called a "partial derivative", meaning that the next information exists on either the x or y axis, and the real information we need from the term after the inverse six is the slope. In this case, the two terms that follow the partial derivatives are the string's spacetime coordinates on the 'a' axis and the 'b' axis.

The Full Equation

$$S_{\text{Polyakov}} = -\frac{T}{2} \int d^2\sigma \sqrt{-h}\, h^{ab} \partial_a X^\mu \partial_b X_\mu$$

In mathematical transliteration:

THE POLYAKOV ACTION IS EXACTLY HALF OF THE NEGATIVE STRING TENSION MULTIPLIED BY THE INTEGRAL OF THE WORLDSHEET AND THE VOLUME ELEMENT OF THE WORLDSHEET AND THE INVERSE WORLDSHEET METRIC AND THE PARTIAL DERIVATIVE OF THE STRING'S COORDINATES OVER ONE DIMENSION [LABELED 'a'] AND THE PARTIAL DERIVATIVE OF THE STRING'S COORDINATES OVER [ANOTHER] ONE DIMENSION [LABELED 'b'].

In plain English:

THE POLYAKOV ACTION IS NEGATIVELY AFFECTED BY THE [VALUE OF HALF THE] STRING TENSION, BUT THE ENTIRE AREA SWEPT OUT BY THE STRING IS INTEGRATED WITH THE STRING'S EXISTENTIAL EFFECT ON THE GEOMETRY OF THE WORLD STRING AND THE SLOPES OF THE STRING'S MOVEMENT ON THE WORLD SHEET.

The world sheet is affected by the movement of the string through three major forms: the tension affects the string in a -2:1 string tension to world-sheet ratio, the string's existence affects the geometry of the world-sheet, and the string's movement on both the x and y axes dramatically affects the world-sheet.

Through both actions, we can mathematically understand that the fundamental strings in String Theory affect their environment and are affected by their environment.

Euler-Lagrange Equations

The Euler-Lagrange equations come from a rule that helps us find out how things move. In string theory, they tell us how the positions of the string change as time goes on. The Euler-Lagrange equations provide a systematic way to derive the equations of motion from an action principle, making them a powerful tool in theoretical physics.

Mathematical Terms

Lagrangian (L): This is a function that represents the difference between the kinetic and potential energies of a system. In the context of string theory, it is derived from the chosen action (either Nambu-Goto or Polyakov) and depends on the string's coordinates and their derivatives.

Coordinates (x): These represent the position of the string in spacetime.

The derivative of x ($\dot{x}$): This represents the derivative of x with respect to time

Time (t): You know what time is.

Derivative ($\partial L / \partial x$): This represents the derivative of the Lagrangian with respect to the string's coordinates. It appears in the Euler-Lagrange equations and determines how the coordinates evolve dynamically.

Variation (δ): The changes in a variable.

Full Equations

$$S = \int L(x, \dot{x}, t)dt$$

This one doesn't need a formal mathematical transliteration. The action (**S**) for a system is defined as the integral ($\int$) of the Langrangian (**L**) over a series that includes coordinates, derivatives of the coordinates, and time. The integral also includes the derivative of time. The reasoning behind why this works is not important, but we need to trust that very smart people worked on this and found that the math does indeed work out. You may refuse to believe this reasoning because it's based on the trust that the way we understand the universe will continue to be understood in this way. If that's the case, I advise you to treat this math in the same way that doctors treat anesthesia. We can easily understand its function, but understanding why it works is so complicated, it's not worth looking into.

Anyway, let's use this equation as our base and add the variation in the action due to small changes in the path of the string's movement. Mathematically, we're also going to partially derive the Langrangian equation so that it's easier to calculate with the variation.

$$\delta S = \int \left(\frac{\partial L}{\partial x} \delta x + \frac{\partial L}{\partial \dot{x}} \delta \dot{x} \right) dt$$

The variation in the action is a function of the integral of the [partially-derived] variation of the coordinates added to the [partially-derived] variation of the derivative of the coordinates; all integrated with the derivative of time. Essentially, we're in the inbetween phase, where the math is abstract and purely logical. Let's keep moving and follow the next logical step. Don't be intimidated if the equation looks different next time we see it. For all intents and purposes, we're essentially converting **5X + 50 = 100** into **X = 10**. It's simplifying the equation as best as we can. This process is called minimization.

To find the true path of the system, we require absolutely no variation in the action, meaning that the variation of S must equal 0, so we must simplify and set it equal to 0.

$$\frac{d}{dt}\left(\frac{\partial L}{\partial \dot{x}}\right) - \frac{\partial L}{\partial x} = 0$$

All this does is mathematically explain the dynamical behavior of the system and describes how the system's position evolves over time.

Stringematics

The equation of motion for the string comes from using the Euler-Lagrange equations with either the Nambu-Goto or Polyakov action. It tells us exactly how the string moves in space and time and what it does. This provides a precise description of how strings propagate in spacetime, both classically and quantum mechanically, and forms the basis for understanding various phenomena in string theory.

Mathematical Terms

Equation of Motion: This is a differential equation that describes the evolution of the string's coordinates over time. It is obtained by applying the Euler-Lagrange equations to the chosen action and represents the fundamental dynamics of the string.

The String's Coordinates (X^μ): This represents the string's location. μ can be any dimension, including time.

Full Equation

$$\frac{\partial \mathcal{L}}{\partial X^\mu} - \frac{\partial}{\partial \sigma^\alpha} \left(\frac{\partial \mathcal{L}}{\partial \left(\frac{\partial X^\mu}{\partial \sigma^\alpha} \right)} \right) = 0.$$

The sum of these three partial derivatives is zero. Let's name these three partial derivatives to avoid being confused.

From left to right, Bob subtracted by AJ = 0.

AJ, in our case, is the shortened version of Aaron-Jacob. Aaron-Jacob is the combined expression of the Andrew of Jacob (the partial derivative of a partial derivative).

The variation of an equation with respect to something is equal to the variation of the same equation with respect to something else. That something else is then differentiated with respect to a third something. (The third something isn't the same but it is related to the second something).

Stringematics sets the variation of the Lagrangian equation with respect to the string's coordinates in spacetime equal to the variation of the Lagrangian with respect to the rates of change of the coordinates on the worldsheet, which are then differentiated with respect to the coordinates on the worldsheet itself, all resulting in zero. The partial derivative of the Langrangian is subtracted by the partial derivative of the partial derivative of Langrangian changes being influenced by the rate of change of the worldsheet coordinates.

If that's tough to understand, let's go back to the name analogy.

If you drive forward at a constant speed, you're not accelerating. You can physically feel the lack of acceleration by being perfectly comfortable in your seat. If you were to speed up, you accelerate and you can physically feel pushed back in your chair. It's not the speed that you feel, it's the acceleration. When it comes to the relationship between worldsheet coordinates (where the string is) and the complicated equation called a Langrangian, what affects the equation is not the changing coordinates, it's the rate of the change in the coordinates. The equation doesn't change if the speed is constant. It changes when the speed changes. So, if the speed remains constant, Jacob writes it down and analyzes it. Jacob tries to explain it to the rest of the class, but it's so complicated that Aaron takes Jacob's analysis and re-explains it in a simpler, more digestible method. This new analysis is called AJ. While this is going on, Bob writes down some information about the variation of the Langrangian equation and explains it. As it turns out, Bob's explanation and AJ's explanation are equal, so if AJ were to be subtracted from Bob, it would equal zero.

This is all to say that the string's motion, as long as it doesn't accelerate or decelerate, can be analyzed; and the entire motion of the string follows a specific, understandable path determined by the action chosen.

We have just determined precisely how the string moves through spacetime according to the principles in String Theory.

Combining this understanding of string motion with our understanding of string vibration and higher-level string interaction, we can build the puzzle of how our universe works according to science's theory of everything.

—

Review

This is a short review of the topics we covered in String Theory and how they interact with each other to form a scientific understanding of the universe.

At the heart of String Theory lies the elegant description of strings as extended objects vibrating in spacetime. String Theory challenges the traditional point particle paradigm by proposing that fundamental particles are actually tiny, vibrating strings with extended structure, leading to a new framework for understanding the universe at its most fundamental level.

String Theory's embrace of extra dimensions offers a compelling resolution to longstanding puzzles in theoretical physics. Through the compactification of these additional dimensions, we witness the emergence of diverse geometries, each encoding distinctive physical phenomena. From Calabi-Yau manifolds (in quantum physics) to orbifolds (in classical physics), the rich tapestry of possible geometries holds the promise of explaining the hierarchical structure of particle masses and couplings.

Duality phenomena lie at the heart of String Theory, transcending traditional notions of particle interactions and spacetime geometry. From T-duality and S-duality to U-duality (both T & S), these symmetries unveil hidden connections between seemingly disparate string theories, ushering in a profound shift in our understanding of fundamental physics. Duality in String Theory helps us see how different versions of the theory are actually connected, like different sides of the same coin. It's like finding out that two seemingly different video games are actually just different levels of the same game. This gives us clues that there might be a single, deeper theory that explains everything in a more fundamental way.

The scattering amplitudes of String Theory provide a window into the microscopic structure of spacetime, revealing intricate patterns of interactions among fundamental strings. By harnessing powerful mathematical techniques such as worldsheet conformal field theory and Riemann surface integrals, we unravel the intricate web of Feynman diagrams that characterize string scattering processes. These amplitudes encode a wealth of information about the underlying String Theory, offering a bridge between theoretical predictions and experimental observations.

Conformal field theory serves as the mathematical backbone of String Theory, providing a powerful framework for understanding the dynamics of strings on their worldsheet. Through the lens of conformal symmetry, we gain deep insights into the renormalization group flow, operator product expansions, and the structure of correlation functions. This profound connection between conformal field theory and String Theory underlies many of the remarkable properties that distinguish String Theory from conventional quantum field theories.

By quantizing the string's degrees of freedom, we uncover a spectrum of vibrational modes that encode the particle spectrum observed in nature. This profound shift lays the groundwork for a unified description of gravity and the other fundamental forces within a single theoretical framework.

The equations of motion governing these strings encapsulate their dynamics, dictating how they propagate and interact. Through the rich interplay between geometry and dynamics, these equations reveal the profound unity underlying the fundamental forces of nature.

String Theory stands as a monument to human ingenuity, offering a compelling vision of the fundamental fabric of reality. Through its intricate web of concepts, from string equations of motion to conformal field theory, String Theory weaves together the disparate threads of quantum mechanics and general relativity into a unified tapestry.

While challenges remain on the path towards a complete understanding, the journey into the depths of String Theory continues to inspire generations of physicists to push the boundaries of knowledge and explore the mysteries of the cosmos.

I believe the author and philosopher, Alexander McKechnie, said it best.

"*Edgar Dean Mitchell was one of the twelve astronauts to walk on the moon, and he said the most amazing part of the trip was the return journey, when he was looking out the window of the capsule and he could see the Earth, the Moon, and the Sun, and he suddenly realized that every molecule in the spacecraft in his body and in the other astronauts' bodies had all originated from some ancient star. And he had this overwhelming sense of unity. It was all the same Lego bricks; all part of the same game, the same cosmic terms of service.*

And it's no different for you and I. Just having thoughts in the first place is made possible by electromagnetism conveying signals between neurons in our brains plus holding our molecules together, as well as the strong interaction kindly keeping the nucleus of our atoms, specifically the protons and neutrons, in place. Meanwhile, the curvature of spacetime, gravity, has been casually keeping us from leaving the ground like Balloon Boy and going for a quick wander through a passing jet engine. Meanwhile, the weak force has been quietly keeping quarks transmuting, regulating the nuclear fusion that powers the stars, some of which billions of years ago prototyped all the Carbon, Nitrogen, and Oxygen in our bodies, allowing us to exist in the first place. And all of this has been facilitated by the fundamental constants of nature: obeying the speed of light, gravitational constant, and all the rest - the buttons the universe has done her coat up with.

...[I hate the notion that] the world is boring and everything's been discovered. Oh, has it? Has it really? Oh, I must have been on the toilet when that particular ontological memo came through. Isn't it nicer and just more honest in a way to admit that we don't have a [scientific] handle on anything yet, that there's nothing normal about reality, [that scientifically, it's] just an insane jigsaw puzzle devised by a madman that's persisted long enough to accept as routine. And in a predictably ungrateful fashion, we still somehow invented a word for boredom.

...Maybe work is bad or you're in a pinch or whatever, and I'm really sorry to hear that, but may I recommend that it is possible to put stuff into perspective, just for a moment, by remembering that every atom in your body is the direct result of universal laws we have no idea to the origin of, that there is in plain sight a mystery called everything, and nothing is self-evident. And really, if we're honest, we don't even have a clue what reality is doing here in the first place".

JUDAISM

Orthodox Judaism, a branch of Judaism, firmly believes in monotheism, rejecting the idea of multiple gods.

Within its rationalist framework, there's a clear distinction between priorities, whether they be rituals or prayers. This important argument fostered a logical understanding of Jewish principles, nurturing the development of scientific reasoning, especially after the denominational split between Orthodox & Reform.

Interestingly, Hasidism (a denomination of Orthodox Judaism), despite its limited scientific knowledge during its inception, inadvertently echoed certain modern scientific consensus views through its various additions to Judaic practices.

As a whole, Judaism emphasizes the concept of everything being interconnected within one Divine entity, highlighting the fundamental nature of our connection to it. By applying mathematical axioms rooted in Orthodox Jewish principles, we can observe how the logical structure of Judaism aligns with modern mathematical logic and the overall connection between the two fields.

—

Metaphysics

Let's get deep.

How does one describe a banana?

Long.

Yeah.

Yellow.

Sometimes.

But those are just adjectives, just appearances. There has to be something behind those appearances; something that makes a banana real. As it turns out, there are tons of examples of phenomena that have existed seemingly forever, that we interact with all the time, but science didn't discover until relatively recently. Stars have been emitting X-rays for long before we discovered their existence. So, logically, there must be a world of appearances, where bananas can be yellow, and a different world, where bananas can exist without appearance and things are only as they are - a world of ultimate reality.

The parts of you that make you exist in the world of appearances are constantly replaced. Cells grow, divide, and die. In the world of appearances, you are a conglomerate entity of your parts, but your physical parts are constantly replaced. Even your thoughts are constantly replaced. If you're defined by your thoughts, then each time you have a new thought and forget the old one, aren't you a new person?

But you do exist.

The concept of traffic is not a physical thing that you can touch, but it exists because more cars enter a part of a road than the cars leaving that part of a road. You are like a road with a (mostly) consistent replacement of cars. Though your parts are replaced, the code of your existence, your DNA, remains the same, creating a physical entity from the patterns of replication. And the same is true in mental patterns. You are not defined by your one-time thought, but as an entity from the patterns of your constantly changing thoughts.

So, which of the patterns (physical and mental) is more real? What is a human itself, not in the world of appearances, but in the world of ultimate reality. What makes you real?

You are, as the author and philosopher Alexander McKechnie wrote, "*a matter pattern that matters*".

Judaism, specifically the Orthodox denomination, answers these metaphysical questions in a way that is internally coherent. In Orthodox Jewish understanding, there exists a world of ultimate reality that we don't live in, and there is something special about humanity; that we are the connection between the two worlds of reality, and that connection defines how everything exists and what the meaning of life truly is.

To understand Orthodox Judaism, we must start with the essence of Judaism, the ultimate rejection of polytheism. Afterward, we discuss the origin of Orthodox-specific Judaism, with a focus on Hasidism*. This gives us a baseline to understand some of the great concepts in Hassidic Judaism. The next chapter, The Big Relationship, is not difficult to understand conceptually, but introduces the act of adding faith-based axioms, which is much more difficult to grasp. After understanding (a) the great concepts and (b) the act of using axioms, we can then define the logic built into Judaism. The next section, Underlying Logic, provides axiomatically laden proofs within the confines of Jewish logic, similar to the mathematical equations in Stringematics.

* The focus of this section is on Hasidism because it's the least scientific-accepting common denomination of Orthodox Judaism. Whenever the modern scientific consensus disagrees with the Torah, Hasidic Jews generally assume the modern scientific consensus to be incorrect because the Torah is infallible. This means that any and all parallels between Hasidism and modern physics should be studied carefully, as they may indicate a shared theory of everything. Parallels between the understanding of the universe in Modern-Orthodox (Modox) Judaism are immaterial because Modox Jews generally interpret Torah in such a way that allows for modern physics to make sense. For example, many Modox Jews believe that the understanding of Hashem's creation of the universe can both be six days and billions of years because the six days may not be our common understanding of days.

Overall, this section is designed to establish a thorough understanding of Judaism such that the comparison between it and String Theory appears natural and earned; slowly moving from the purely conceptual to the purely logical.

Judaism

Judaism is the world's oldest monotheistic religion, dating back over 3,500 years. It's the faith, culture, and way of life of the Jewish people, who trace their ancestry back to the ancient Israelites. At the heart of Judaism is the belief in one God who created the universe and who revealed His laws and commandments to the Jewish people through mass revelation and prophets, primarily documented in the Hebrew Bible, known as the Tanakh. Central to Judaism are the teachings and commandments found in the Torah, which consists of the first five books of the Hebrew Bible: Bereshit (Genesis), Shemot (Exodus), Vayikra (Leviticus), Bamidbar (Numbers), and Devarim (Deuteronomy). These commandments cover various aspects of life, including moral and ethical behavior, rituals, and dietary laws.

Orthodox Judaism is one of the major streams or denominations within Judaism, known for its adherence to traditional Jewish beliefs, practices, and interpretations of Jewish law, known as Halakha. Orthodox Jews typically observe Jewish law meticulously, including dietary laws (keeping kosher), observing the Sabbath (Shabbat), and following traditional prayer rituals. Orthodox Judaism places a strong emphasis on the study of Torah and Talmud, which are foundational texts of Jewish law and tradition. Education, particularly religious education, is highly valued within Orthodox communities, and many Orthodox Jews attend yeshivas (religious schools) to study Jewish texts in-depth. Orthodox Judaism also tends to maintain traditional gender roles within religious practice, with distinct roles for men and women in prayer and communal life.

Overall, Orthodox Judaism emphasizes the preservation of Jewish tradition and continuity with the practices of previous generations, striving to live in accordance with the laws and customs passed down through centuries of Jewish history.

Antisemitism

Hatred of Jews appears to be so ubiquitous in worldwide history, it might as well be written within the strands making up the fabric of the universe, and if so, maybe there's something fundamentally different between Jews and everyone else. Even if not embedded within the universe, Jews and Judaism have been at the forefront of worldwide everything. It's not a conspiracy theory to note that Jews have been disproportionately successful for thousands of years, leading worldwide changes and having major roles in almost every historical event. What is it about Jews and Judaism that makes Jews phenomenally successful and vitriolically hated?

In Judaism, the origin of antisemitism is often traced back to the biblical nation of Amalek. According to Jewish tradition, Amalek was an ancient enemy of the Israelites who attacked them shortly after their exodus from Egypt. The Torah recounts the story in Shemot (the Book of Exodus) and Devarim (the Book of Deuteronomy), where Amalek is described as a ruthless and merciless adversary who targeted the Israelites when they were physically vulnerable yet actively engaging in phenomenal miracles. The commandment to remember and eradicate Amalek is central to Jewish theology, as it represents the struggle against evil and oppression. The Torah commands the Israelites to "*blot out the memory of Amalek from under heaven*" (Devarim 25:19), and this commandment is understood to extend beyond the historical context to a broader moral imperative to combat injustice and persecution. Throughout Jewish history, Amalek has been seen as a symbol of antisemitism and the perennial enemy of the Jewish people. The sages of the Talmud and later Jewish commentators interpreted the commandment to eradicate Amalek as a mandate to confront and defeat the enemies of the Jewish people, both physically and spiritually. In contemporary Jewish thought, the concept of Amalek is often invoked to explain the persistence of antisemitism throughout history. Just as Amalek symbolized unprovoked hatred and aggression towards the Israelites, antisemitism is seen as an irrational and deeply ingrained prejudice that continues to manifest itself in various forms.

Throughout history, Jews have often faced discrimination, persecution, and expulsion from various regions. Despite these challenges, Jewish communities have demonstrated resilience and adaptability. Historically, Jews were often excluded from certain professions and land ownership, leading them to pursue occupations like finance, trade, and academia, where they could thrive despite societal restrictions. Jews have faced numerous challenges, including persecution, expulsion, and genocide, but despite these adversities, Jewish communities have demonstrated resilience and adaptability, rebuilding and thriving in the face of adversity.

Education has been highly valued in Jewish tradition for centuries, with a strong emphasis on literacy and scholarship. Jewish communities have historically invested heavily in education, ensuring that Jewish individuals have the skills and knowledge to succeed in various fields. Additionally, Jewish communities have often maintained strong social networks and support systems, which can contribute to success in business, education, and other endeavors. These networks provide opportunities for mentorship, collaboration, and resource-sharing.

Due to their success, but more likely their strong sense of independent community, Jews have been the targets of stereotypes, myths, and conspiracy theories that portray them as greedy, manipulative, or controlling. After all, if you heard that a distant independent community has found disproportionate success and naturally prioritizes others within their community over everyone else, then you have a powerful choice: you could respect and cooperate with this community in the hopes of shared success, or you could internalize your negative feelings about this situation and allow them to control your behavior, inevitably leading to attempts (varied-in-successfulness) at destruction of the distant community.

These negative stereotypes contribute to prejudice, discrimination, and often violence against Jewish individuals and communities. These stereotypes are one of the many warning signs before a nation attempts to severely upend their internal Jewish life, often through expulsion and/or genocide. We see antisemitic stereotypes in the modern day through Islamic nations (who have already killed or kicked out their Jews) and Universities in the western world, with some nations in the western world beginning to accept relatively-small attempts to upend their internal Jewish life.

A Physics Perspective

In physics, we often encounter the idea of fundamental principles governing the universe. Similarly, Judaism revolves around fundamental principles laid out in the Torah, the central text of Judaism, which contains laws, teachings, and narratives of the Jewish people's relationship with the Divine. Just as physics explores the nature of existence, Judaism delves into profound questions about the meaning of life, ethical behavior, and our connection to something greater than ourselves. The concept of God in Judaism can be seen as akin to the underlying forces or laws of the universe that govern existence.

Furthermore, Judaism places a strong emphasis on community and collective responsibility. Just as in physics, where interactions between particles can shape the behavior of systems, Jewish teachings stress the interconnectedness of individuals and the importance of collective action in shaping society. In terms of rituals and observances, Judaism offers a structured framework for spiritual connection and ethical living. Observing mitzvot (commandments) can be likened to following scientific principles or laws that guide behavior and interaction with the world. The Jewish calendar, with its cycle of festivals and observances, reflects a deep understanding of the rhythms of time and nature, echoing the cyclic patterns found in the physical world.

Overall, while physics seeks to understand the material universe through empirical observation and theoretical frameworks, Judaism explores the spiritual dimensions of existence, offering guidance, wisdom, and a sense of belonging to those who follow its teachings. Just as physics seeks to uncover the mysteries of the cosmos, Judaism invites its adherents to explore the mysteries of the Divine and their place within the larger cosmic order.

—

An Orthodox Origin

This is the history of Orthodox Judaism, prioritizing Torah study, Jewish ritual, and prayer.

Rational Monotheism

A.   Rationality is absurdly powerful.

B.   In Jewish understanding, everything intrinsically follows one creationary force above all.

Monotheism, the belief in one God, stands as the cornerstone of Judaism, the world's oldest monotheistic religion. Throughout history, Judaism has withstood the test of time, remaining resilient amidst various challenges and changes. At its core lies the belief in a single, omnipotent, and omnipresent God. This monotheism found in Judaism is inherently rational and reasonable.

First and foremost, monotheism in Judaism is rational because it provides a coherent framework for understanding the universe. The concept of one supreme being simplifies the understanding of the cosmos, offering a singular source of existence and order. This simplicity aligns with Occam's Razor, a principle in philosophy advocating for the simplest explanation when faced with competing hypotheses. In monotheism, there is no need to juggle multiple gods with conflicting attributes and agendas. Instead, there is a unified force governing all aspects of creation, making sense of the complexity and variety observed in the world.

Furthermore, monotheism in Judaism is reasonable as it fosters intellectual inquiry and critical thinking. Unlike polytheistic belief systems where gods may act arbitrarily or whimsically, monotheism posits a rational deity whose actions are governed by reason and purpose. This encourages believers to seek understanding through contemplation, study, and discourse. In Jewish tradition, the pursuit of knowledge, or "*Chochmah*," is highly valued, reflecting a deep respect for rational inquiry. By attributing the order and design of the universe to a single Divine intellect, Judaism provides a foundation for scientific exploration and philosophical inquiry.

The monotheism in Judaism offers a morally coherent worldview. A singular, righteous God serves as the ultimate moral authority, providing a basis for ethical behavior and justice. The *Aseret Hadibrot* (Ten Commandments) and other moral teachings in Judaism derive their authority from this monotheistic framework, emphasizing the inherent dignity and worth of every individual. This belief in a just and compassionate God instills a sense of responsibility towards others and motivates adherents to strive for righteousness and moral integrity.

We can see this in the Judeo-Christian design of the court system of the United States. In the US, an alleged criminal is innocent until proven guilty, and in the criminal context, the state must prove guilt beyond a shadow of a doubt. If we began with a presumption of guilt, the human tendency toward confirmation bias would result in the vast majority of alleged criminals being sentenced as criminals. Whereas, since we begin with a presumption of innocence, the human tendency toward most biases should result in favorable rulings toward those who are truly innocent. The presumption of innocence denotes the limit of human objectivity. There's a sound argument that the modern US criminal justice system is unjust in some capacity, but only the original design is material to the Jewish understanding of human subjectivity. Thus, monotheism in Judaism not only appeals to reason but also provides a moral compass for navigating the complexities of human existence.

Additionally, the historical resilience of Judaism underscores the rationality of its monotheistic beliefs. Despite facing persecution, exile, and adversity throughout its history, Judaism has endured, maintaining its monotheistic faith amidst changing cultural and political landscapes. This resilience suggests that monotheism in Judaism is not merely a product of cultural conditioning or superstition but is rooted in a profound understanding of human nature and the Divine. The enduring appeal of monotheism reflects its ability to provide solace, meaning, and purpose in the face of life's uncertainties and challenges.

Overall, the monotheism found in Judaism is inherently rational and reasonable, offering a coherent framework for understanding the universe, fostering intellectual inquiry, providing a moral compass, and demonstrating historical resilience. By embracing the belief in one God, Judaism presents a worldview that is both intellectually satisfying and spiritually fulfilling. As humanity continues to grapple with questions of existence and meaning, the rationality of monotheism in Judaism offers timeless insights into the nature of reality and the human condition.

Creation to the 1700s

Ancient Origins (X - 500 BCE)

According to Jewish understanding, Hashem created the universe ex nihilo, out of nothing, through Divine will and intentionality.

The Book of Bereshit (Genesis), the first book of the Torah, outlines the creation story. It describes how Hashem (G-D) formed the world in six days, culminating in the creation of humanity, with Adam and Eve as the first human beings. This narrative emphasizes Hashem's role as the ultimate Creator and the source of all existence. Following the creation narrative, Judaism highlights the early interactions between Hashem and humanity, particularly through figures like Adam, Chava (Eve), Cain, and Hevel (Abel). These stories illustrate fundamental moral and ethical lessons, such as the consequences of disobedience and the importance of righteousness. The narrative then progresses to focus on Noah and the Great Flood, which symbolizes Divine judgment and purification. Noah is portrayed as a righteous individual who finds favor in the eyes of Hashem, leading to his survival along with his family and representatives of all living creatures.

The next significant figure in Jewish tradition is Abraham. He is considered the first patriarch of the Jewish people and is revered for his unwavering faith and obedience to Hashem. The covenant established between Abraham and Hashem is a cornerstone of Judaism, symbolizing a sacred agreement in which Hashem promises to bless Abraham and his descendants, and Abraham commits to serving and following Hashem's commandments. This establishes the first step in the progression of the Divine-human connection. Abraham's journey is marked by various trials and tests of faith, including his willingness to sacrifice his son Isaac as commanded by God—a test that demonstrates his absolute devotion to Hashem. Through Abraham, Judaism emphasizes the importance of faith, righteousness, and the enduring covenant between God and the Jewish people.

Following this pact, Abraham's descendants, known as the Israelites, migrated to Egypt. However, their time in Egypt was marked by enslavement and hardship. Eventually, under the leadership of Moses, they embarked on a journey to freedom known as the Exodus. This event, with its dramatic escape from bondage and pursuit by the Egyptian army, is one of the most foundational narratives in Jewish history, a transition from servitude of mankind to servitude of Hashem. A pivotal moment in Jewish tradition occurred when Moses ascended Mount Sinai and received the Torah from Hashem. The Torah, which includes the first five books of the Hebrew Bible, is considered the central text of Judaism. It contains not only religious laws (mitzvot) but also ethical teachings, narratives, and guidelines for Jewish life. The giving of the Torah at Mount Sinai is considered a crucial event as it claims mass revelation and establishes the framework for Jewish beliefs, practices, and moral principles.

Jewish Kingdoms (c. 1200 BCE - 586 BCE)

After the life of Moses, the Jewish people, known as B'nei Yisrael (Children of Israel - Israelites), then conquered the land of Israel. B'nei Yisrael began the Kingdom of Israel, before splitting between the Kingdom of Israel and the Kingdom of Judah. Canaan, the original name for the land of Israel, now consisted of the Kingdom of Israel in the north and the Kingdom of Judah in the south. In fact, the term "Jew" is an anglicized version of Judean, an individual from the land of Judah. This division occurred after the reign of King Solomon, the son of King David, who is credited with the construction of the First Temple in Jerusalem. This temple became the central religious sanctuary for the B'nei Yisrael, where they conducted worship and offered sacrifices according to the laws prescribed in the Torah.

However, the unity of the Israelite kingdoms did not last long. Internal strife and external pressures led to their eventual downfall. The Kingdom of Israel faced conquest by the Assyrian Empire in 722 BCE, leading to the exile of many Israelites and the dispersion of the population. The Kingdom of Judah managed to survive for a while longer, but it too faced threats from neighboring empires.

In 586 BCE, the Babylonians, under King Nebuchadnezzar II, conquered Jerusalem and destroyed the First Temple. This event, known as the Babylonian Exile, was a pivotal moment in Jewish history. Many Judeans were taken into captivity in Babylon, where they lived as exiles for several decades. This period of exile had a profound impact on Jewish identity, as it forced the people to grapple with questions of faith, identity, and their relationship with Hashem.

Exile and Return (c. 586 BCE - 515 BCE)

The Babylonian Exile saw many Jews deported, but despite the destruction of the First Temple and the exile, the Jewish people managed to maintain their religious and cultural identity. Eventually, with the rise of the Persian Empire and the decree of King Cyrus allowing the Jews to return to their homeland, the Second Temple was built in Jerusalem, marking a new chapter in Jewish history.

Classical Era (c. 333 BCE - 70 CE)

The influence of Hellenistic (Greek-influenced) culture intensified following the conquests of Alexander the Great. This cultural shift sparked tensions as traditional Jewish practices clashed with Hellenistic norms and values. Despite occasional resistance, including the Maccabean Revolt of 165 BCE, which briefly secured Jewish independence, the overall trajectory was one of increasing assimilation and accommodation to Hellenistic influences. However, the Roman conquest in 63 BCE marked a significant turning point. With Roman rule came a series of
110

challenges to Jewish autonomy and religious practices. Ultimately, these tensions culminated in the devastating event of the destruction of the Second Temple in 70 CE.

Rather than solely attributing the destruction of the Second Temple to external forces, it's important to acknowledge the internal divisions and faithlessness within the Jewish community at the time. These internal conflicts weakened the community's cohesion and resilience, contributing to its vulnerability to external threats and ultimately leading to the tragic loss of the Second Temple.

Diaspora & Rabbinic Judaism (c. 70 CE - 500 CE)

With the loss of the Second Temple, Judaism shifted towards Rabbinic Judaism. The compilation of the Mishnah and the Gemara laid the foundation for the Talmud, a central text of Jewish law and tradition. The Jewish diaspora spread across the Roman Empire and then spread around the world.

Medieval Period (500 CE - 1500 CE)

During the Middle Ages, Judaism experienced a complex tapestry of both cultural flourishing and persecution. Jewish communities were scattered throughout various regions, including Spain, the Middle East, and parts of Europe. Despite facing periodic persecution, Jews made significant intellectual and cultural contributions to society.

In Spain, particularly during the Golden Age of Jewish culture in the medieval period (around the 10th to 12th centuries), Jewish scholars thrived in an environment of relative tolerance under Muslim rule. This period saw the emergence of renowned Jewish thinkers like Maimonides, who made groundbreaking contributions to philosophy, medicine, and Jewish legal thought. However, this period of relative tolerance was not without its challenges. The Reconquista, the Christian reconquest of Spain, led to the gradual erosion of Jewish rights and freedoms. Eventually, with the culmination of the Spanish Inquisition in 1492, Jews faced expulsion from Spain unless they converted to Christianity. Many chose exile rather than abandoning their faith, leading to significant upheaval within Jewish communities.

In other parts of Europe, Jews faced similar challenges. The Crusades, in an attempt to reclaim biblical Israel from Muslim control, often resulted in violence against Jewish communities along the route to the Holy Land. Additionally, Jews were frequently scapegoated during times of social unrest, leading to pogroms and forced expulsions in various regions. Despite these hardships, Jewish scholarship continued to thrive. The Middle East, particularly centers like Baghdad and Cairo, remained important hubs of Jewish intellectual activity. Jewish scholars in these regions made significant contributions to fields such as philosophy, mathematics, and biblical commentary.

Expulsion and Renaissance (1500s - 1600s)

The Spanish Expulsion of 1492 forced many Jews to leave Spain. Jewish communities found somewhat of a refuge in Ottoman Empire territories and other parts of Europe. The Renaissance saw renewed interest in Jewish culture, with figures like Baruch Spinoza (Benedictus de Spinoza) engaging in philosophical discussions. There were many local persecutions of Jews, but nothing of worldwide significance during this time.

Cultural Expansion & Reform (1600s - 1700s)

Jewish communities experienced cultural and economic growth in places like Amsterdam and Venice. The controversial Jewish philosopher, Moses Mendelssohn, emerged during the Enlightenment, advocating for Jewish integration and equal rights, eventually starting the movement that would become known as Progressive Judaism or Reform.

The following subsection is a detailed description of what happened to bring about the rise in Hasidism, Misnagdim, Reform, and eventual Orthodox Judaism.

The Priority Problem

Hasidism

Thousands of years of worldwide persecution of Jews just trying to follow Judaic law resulted in a Jewish generational depression. Jews followed religious laws strictly, but miserably.

Hasidic Judaism originated as a rejection of the depressional style of strictly following religious laws. According to Hasidism, one must strictly follow religious laws, but instead of following the laws silently and minimally, one must follow the laws with deep enthusiasm and energetic prayer. This movement split Judaism into two camps: Hasidism and Misnagdim. The Misnagdim worried that Hasidism is another false messianic movement centered around high-level rabbis.

Hasidim proved their worth and loyalty to Judaism by adding more concepts and deeper understandings centered around Judaism, instead of Christianity, which, according to Jewish understanding, is an official false messianic movement. Hassids also increased the number of Jewish printing presses by adding 18 new presses for a total of 20. It can easily be argued that through the Hassidic understanding of using very sharp knives for butchery, the butchers would join the movement, and thereby spread Hasidism through towns, as everybody would need to meet the butcher. Jewish guilds designed around fulfilling a specific mitzvah were penetrated by Hassids, enhancing the process of doing mitzvot. The rivalry between the Misnagdim and the Hasidism ended when Reform Judaism sprouted, arguably destroying the fabric of following religious laws in favor of following the general vibe. The Misnagdim and Hasidism merged together to form what we know as Orthodox Judaism today.

Misnagdim (Action)

The Misnagdim, known as the opponents of the Chasidic (Hasidic) movement, were a prominent faction within Judaism that emerged in Eastern Europe during the 18th century. Their emergence was largely a response to the growing influence of Chasidic teachings and practices. The Misnagdim held distinct theological and ideological positions that set them apart from the Chasidim.

Primarily, the Misnagdim opposed the Chasidic movement due to perceived deviations in religious practice, mysticism, and authority. They advocated for a more traditionalist interpretation of Judaism, emphasizing rigorous Talmudic study, adherence to established liturgical practices, and a cautious approach towards mystical teachings. The Misnagdim were deeply entrenched in the intellectual and religious life of Eastern European Jewry. They established yeshivas (traditional Jewish schools) and centers of learning, where they promoted their doctrinal views and engaged in scholarly debates. Their influence extended beyond academic circles, shaping the religious identity and communal practices of Jewish communities in the region. Throughout the 18th and 19th centuries, the relationship between the Misnagdim and the Chasidic communities was characterized by tension and conflict. Debates over theological doctrine, ritual observance, and communal leadership often led to heated disputes and occasional violence.

Despite their opposition to Hasidism, the Misnagdim played a significant role in preserving traditional Jewish religious norms and practices in Eastern Europe. Their commitment to Talmudic scholarship and their staunch defense of established religious authority contributed to the diversity and richness of Jewish religious life in the region.

114

Reform (The General Vibe)

The rise of the Enlightenment eventually started the movement that would become known as Progressive Judaism or Reform, but what is the Enlightenment?

The Enlightenment in Jewish history, also known as Haskalah, was a significant intellectual and cultural movement that emerged in the late 18th and early 19th centuries. It was influenced by the broader European Enlightenment, which promoted rationality, secularism, and individualism. The Jewish Enlightenment sought to modernize Jewish life by advocating for secular education, integration into broader society, and the adoption of secular knowledge and values. It challenged traditional religious authority and practices, encouraging critical thinking and the pursuit of knowledge beyond religious texts. Some Jewish intellectuals began to promote secular education, linguistic and cultural assimilation, and engagement with secular philosophy and literature. The Jewish Enlightenment facilitated a greater integration of Jews into secular society, leading to changes in religious practices, social norms, and communal organization.

This eventually created a new sect of Judaism, one in which Jews need not strictly follow religious laws, called Reform (also known as Liberal or Progressive Judaism). The existence of Reform Judaism was seen as an insult to traditional Jews in that according to the traditional Jews, it was destroying the fabric of Judaism. Reform Jews thought they were comfortable where they were, so they dropped the idea of "returning to Jerusalem", a cornerstone of jewish thought, in favor of staying in Germany. Reform Jews also allowed for Jewish identities to be split in that those who were less religious could be considered "culturally" or "spiritually" Jewish because one didn't have to follow the laws; only the spirit of them. This promptly resulted in the merging of the two other sects. Those sects wanted to distinguish themselves from a rapidly-increasing population of Reform Jews, and wanted to inform others that the two sects' version of Judaism was the original and Reform was unorthodox, so they called their newly-merged sect Orthodox.

Haskala sparked debates within Jewish communities about the balance between tradition and modernity, faith and reason, and Jewish particularism and universalism. Orthodox Jews strongly resisted the movement, reaffirming traditional religious beliefs and practices in response to the perceived threats of assimilation and secularization.

–

Hasidic Concepts

The Notion of Motion

Hasidic Judaism, a mystical and fervent branch of Orthodox Judaism, encompasses a rich tapestry of beliefs and practices deeply rooted in Jewish tradition. At the heart of Hasidic thought lies the concept of constant movement, a dynamic and transformative understanding of spiritual growth and Divine interaction. We will delve into the intricate layers of this concept within Hasidic Judaism, exploring its philosophical underpinnings, its practical manifestations, and its profound implications for the individual and the community.

Central to the notion of constant movement in Hasidic Judaism is the dynamic relationship between the individual and the Divine. Hasidic teachings emphasize the idea of deveikut, or cleaving to God, as the ultimate goal of spiritual striving. This concept posits that the human soul is in a perpetual state of ascent towards greater closeness to the Divine. It suggests that spiritual growth is not static but rather an ongoing journey characterized by continuous movement and progression. This movement is not linear but cyclical, marked by peaks and valleys, moments of illumination and periods of darkness. It reflects the ebb and flow of the soul's quest for union with the Divine, encompassing both ecstatic moments of connection and mundane routines of daily life.

Furthermore, constant movement in Hasidic Judaism encompasses the cyclical nature of time and the rhythms of the natural world. Hasidic masters often draw parallels between the seasons of the year and the spiritual seasons of the soul. Just as the natural world undergoes cycles of growth, decay, and renewal, so too does the human soul experience cycles of spiritual ascent, descent, and transformation. The Hasidic calendar is replete with festivals, fast days, and other sacred occasions that mark the passage of time and invite individuals to engage in introspection, repentance, and renewal. Each moment in time is seen as pregnant with potential for spiritual growth, offering opportunities for individuals to deepen their connection to the Divine and elevate their consciousness to higher realms.

The constant movement in Hasidic Judaism is manifested through dynamic modes of worship and prayer. Hasidic communities engage in lively and spirited forms of communal prayer, characterized by fervent melodies, ecstatic dancing, and heartfelt supplications. These practices are designed to uplift the soul and facilitate moments of spiritual transcendence. Hasidic prayer is not merely a rote recitation of words but a heartfelt dialogue with the Divine, infused with passion, sincerity, and longing. Through prayer, individuals are invited to enter into the

Divine presence and experience moments of communion with the sacred.

Additionally, constant movement in Hasidic Judaism is reflected in the emphasis on spiritual growth and self-transformation. Hasidic teachings stress the importance of engaging in daily acts of self-refinement, ethical conduct, and mitzvah observance. The Hasidic path is one of continuous self-examination and inner work, as individuals strive to overcome their egoic tendencies and align themselves more closely with the Divine will. This process of inner transformation is seen as integral to the soul's journey towards deveikut and ultimate union with the Divine.

The notion of constant movement in Hasidic Judaism encapsulates a profound understanding of spiritual growth, Divine interaction, and the human condition. It encompasses the dynamic relationship between the individual and the Divine, the cyclical nature of time and the natural world, dynamic modes of worship and prayer, and the emphasis on spiritual growth and self-transformation. Through the lens of constant movement, Hasidic Judaism offers a powerful framework for navigating the complexities of spiritual life and deepening one's connection to the sacred, and nothing is more appropox of constant motion than the understanding of constant creation.

Constant Creation

According to Hasidic Judaism, creation itself is an active act. Hashem did not just create the world. The Divine is creating the world actively. This is accomplished through a manner of creation that you and I can both do. Picture a table in your mind. That's it. Through the manner of my speech, I created the image of a table in your mind. That exact table doesn't exist in the physical world, but you and I have participated in an act of creation through a non-physical medium. Hasidic Jews understand that Hashem creates the world through speech. It's an active process, meaning that the physical universe is actively being created and changed through the medium of Divine language. Our process of speech involves vibrations of a physical entity creating language that others can understand. This, contends Hasidism, is the same act of creation that Hashem uses; the vibration of a physical entity that is the universe is the active process of Divine creation. Without getting too far ahead of ourselves, that is the same assertion fundamental to String Theory.

Tzimtzum

Imagine the universe as a vast, boundless canvas, filled with infinite potential and possibilities. Now, picture the Divine as the ultimate artist, whose presence permeates every corner of this canvas. According to Hasidic philosophy, the concept of Tzimtzum introduces the idea that before creation, this Divine presence was so overwhelming and all-encompassing that there was no room for anything else to exist. In a sense, it's like a stage with a blindingly bright spotlight; everything else is overshadowed and invisible. However, for creation to occur and for other entities to emerge, there needed to be a sort of "contraction" or "concealment" of this Divine presence. This is where Tzimtzum comes into play. It's as if the artist dims the spotlight, creating space for other elements to come into being. This act of contraction is not a withdrawal or absence of the Divine, but rather a concealment of its overwhelming presence to allow for the existence of a complex and dynamic universe.

Through the lens of Tzimtzum, Hasidic thought explores the profound mysteries of creation and the relationship between the Infinite and the finite. It delves into questions of how the Divine interacts with the world, how seemingly separate entities are still connected to their Divine source, and how the balance between concealment and revelation shapes the unfolding of existence. In essence, Tzimtzum invites us to contemplate the intricate dance between the transcendent and the immanent, the infinite and the finite, as we seek to understand the deeper meanings and purposes behind the universe's existence.

Extra Dimensions

The number and nature of dimensions beyond our own.

Hasidic Judaism, with its rich mystical heritage, provides an intriguing lens through which to explore the significance of extra dimensions. Particularly, the numbers 10 and 26 hold profound importance in Hasidic thought, shedding light on their understanding of the spiritual and metaphysical realms. In exploring the Hasidic perspective on extra dimensions through the significance of the numbers 10 and 26, we encounter a profound synthesis of mystical insight and mathematical speculation. Through the lens of Hasidic mysticism, extra dimensions are not merely abstract concepts but reflections of deeper spiritual truths. The interconnectedness of the sefirot and the Divine unity represented by the Tetragrammaton offer profound insights into the nature of reality and the mysteries of existence. While the exploration of extra dimensions remains a subject of ongoing scientific inquiry, the Hasidic perspective reminds us of the boundless potential for wonder and awe in the quest for understanding the cosmos.

The Significance of 10:

In Hasidic mysticism, the number 10 symbolizes the ten sefirot, or Divine emanations, which form the basis of the Kabbalistic Tree of Life. Each sefirah represents a different aspect of the Divine, ranging from wisdom to compassion, and together they encompass the entirety of creation. Hasidic teachings emphasize the interconnectedness of these sefirot, suggesting a holistic understanding of the universe. From a mathematical perspective, the existence of ten dimensions could be seen as a reflection of this spiritual concept, with each dimension corresponding to a different aspect of reality. Just as the sefirot interact and influence one another, so too could these dimensions intertwine to shape the fabric of existence in ways beyond our comprehension.

Furthermore, the number 10 holds significance in Hasidic numerology as representing completeness or perfection. This notion aligns with the idea of extra dimensions as completing our understanding of the universe, offering a more comprehensive framework for explaining the mysteries of existence. From a Hasidic perspective, the inclusion of extra dimensions could signify a deeper level of harmony and unity within creation, reflecting the Divine order inherent in the cosmos.

The Significance of 26:

In addition to the number 10, the number 26 holds particular significance in Hasidic tradition. It is associated with the Divine name of God, known as the Tetragrammaton, which consists of four Hebrew letters with a numerical value of 26. This name is considered sacred and represents the essence of God's infinite wisdom and power. In Kabbalistic teachings, the Tetragrammaton serves as a symbol of Divine unity and the underlying unity of all existence.

From a mathematical standpoint, the number 26 could be interpreted as indicative of a higher-dimensional reality encompassing the Divine essence. Just as the Tetragrammaton transcends the limitations of human understanding, so too could extra dimensions transcend the confines of our conventional perception of space and time. Hasidic mystics often speak of the ineffable nature of God, suggesting that the Divine presence permeates all dimensions of reality, both seen and unseen.

Modern Moshiach

Hasidic Jews understand that we currently exist in the messianic age. This belief differs from the beliefs within other branches of Orthodox Judaism, in that other Orthodox Jews believe that humanity will have a messianic revelation at an undetermined time in the future, and knowing the exact date is an infohazard, therefore the Hasidic perspective must be based on unclear information. Hasidic Jews disagree in that they understand the signs of Moshiach to be exceedingly clear in the modern day and the process before the ultimate revelation takes a long time, therefore, humanity must be going through that process right now.

The differences in thought between Hasidic Jews and other Orthodox Jews are many, but the underlying belief that the relationship between oneself and Hashem is the defining factor of existence is shared between all sects within Orthodox Judaism.

—

The Big Relationship

An individual's relationship with Hashem is the cornerstone of Jewish faith and identity, shaping every aspect of religious life and practice.

Connectedness

In Judaism, the fundamental relationship with God is often described as a covenant, a sacred agreement between the Divine and the Jewish people. This covenant forms the cornerstone of Jewish faith and identity, shaping every aspect of religious life and practice. At its core, the relationship between God and the Jewish people is rooted in mutual love, trust, and responsibility. According to Jewish tradition, God chose the Jewish people to be a "chosen people," not in the sense of superiority, but rather as a special responsibility to embody and uphold certain values and teachings.Central to this relationship is the concept of obedience to God's commandments, as outlined in the Torah, the sacred scripture of Judaism. Through the observance of mitzvot (commandments), Jews demonstrate their commitment to God and their willingness to live in accordance with Divine teachings.

However, the relationship between God and the Jewish people is not one-sided. It is characterized by a dynamic interplay of love, devotion, and accountability. Just as the Jewish people are called to fulfill their obligations to God, they also believe that God is actively involved in their lives, guiding, protecting, and providing for them. This relationship is further nurtured through prayer, study, and acts of loving-kindness (gemilut chasadim). Through these spiritual practices, Jews seek to deepen their connection to the Divine and cultivate a sense of intimacy and closeness with God. The relationship with God is not limited to individual devotion but extends to the collective identity of the Jewish people as a community.

Throughout history, Jews have experienced periods of exile, persecution, and hardship, yet their faith and resilience have been sustained by the enduring belief in God's presence and promise. In essence, the fundamental relationship with God in Judaism is one of profound love, faith, and commitment, characterized by a reciprocal bond of loyalty and devotion between the Divine and the Jewish people. It is a relationship that transcends time and space, shaping the identity, values, and destiny of the Jewish people throughout history.

Overarching Unity

In the realm of religion and spirituality, Judaism stands as one of the oldest and most profound belief systems in human history. Rooted in millennia of tradition, scripture, and philosophical inquiry, Judaism offers a rich tapestry of theological concepts, ethical principles, and mystical insights. Central to Jewish thought is the notion of a comprehensive worldview, a unified understanding of the universe and humanity's place within it. While Judaism encompasses a wide array of interpretations and perspectives, there is an argument to be made for the existence of an overarching Theory of Everything within its teachings. At the heart of Jewish theology lies the concept of monotheism, the belief in one singular, omnipotent God who is the creator and sustainer of the universe. This foundational principle provides the framework upon which all other theological ideas within Judaism are built.

The unity of God as expressed in the Shema, the central declaration of Jewish faith found in the Torah, epitomizes the singularity and universality of the Divine. Through this lens, all aspects of existence are understood to emanate from and be interconnected by the Divine presence, forming a cohesive and integrated whole. Furthermore, Jewish mysticism, particularly within the Kabbalistic tradition, offers profound insights into the nature of reality and the underlying unity of existence. Kabbalah posits the existence of a Divine emanation known as the Sefirot, through which Hashem's infinite light is manifested and channeled into the material world. These Sefirot form a cosmic framework through which all aspects of existence are interconnected, reflecting the Divine attributes and serving as channels for spiritual energy. In this way, Kabbalah presents a holistic worldview that integrates the physical and spiritual dimensions of reality into a unified whole, offering a comprehensive understanding of existence.

Ethical monotheism, another cornerstone of Jewish thought, emphasizes the moral imperative to live in accordance with Divine will and ethical principles. The commandments outlined in the Torah provide a blueprint for righteous living and guide individuals towards spiritual growth and ethical behavior. Through the observance of mitzvot (commandments) and the cultivation of moral virtues, individuals are called to participate in the ongoing process of tikkun olam, the repair and elevation of the world. This ethical framework not only informs individual conduct but also shapes societal structures and norms, fostering a sense of interconnectedness and communal responsibility.

Additionally, Jewish eschatology offers a vision of ultimate redemption and restoration, wherein the fractured elements of creation are reconciled and harmonized. The concept of mashiach (messiah) represents the culmination of history, a time when justice, peace, and righteousness will reign supreme. This messianic era heralds the realization of God's ultimate plan for creation, wherein all beings will recognize and submit to Divine sovereignty. Through this lens, the disparate threads of human history are woven together into a unified narrative of redemption and fulfillment.

While Judaism encompasses a wide array of beliefs, practices, and interpretations, there exists a cohesive and overarching Theory of Everything within its teachings. Rooted in monotheism, mysticism, ethics, and eschatology, this comprehensive worldview offers a unified understanding of existence and humanity's place within the cosmos. Through the integration of these theological concepts, Judaism presents a holistic framework that illuminates the interconnectedness of all aspects of reality and provides guidance for living a life of meaning, purpose, and righteousness.

Disconnectedness

Non-depression general unhappiness may be a functional failure of your relationship with life. For those that are sad, one should ask them if they are depressed or if their life is bad. Maybe they don't have a romantic partner, a close family, a close friend, a societal function, a higher purpose, or any real way of improving their situation. They may not feel sad in the same way as someone who has all of these does. Someone who has every single one of these should, for all intents and purposes, be at least satisfied with their situation, whereas someone who has none of these should reasonably be expected to be dissatisfied with their situation. We can expect this because the difference between the two is not entirely surface level. There's an underlying connection that people have with life that grants satisfaction and general happiness. The more people connect with life, the happier people generally feel. The way in which people connect with life is through a social community; the tribal attitude of which grants people a sense of belonging. That feeling gives people meaning and drive, and sets the basis for how to be happy in the future. Unfortunately, most people have one or more aspects of their connection with life unfulfilled, and thus, there's a hole in their connection, allowing the feelings of loneliness to balloon and driving away happiness.

In Judaism, the point and meaning of life is to enhance your relationship with Hashem, the process of which establishes a long-term underlying goal and the drive to accomplish it.. Attempting to do so quickly leads to mending the holes in one's relationship with life, which naturally progresses into working hard to have a good life, and very often, the better relationship one has with life and the universe, the higher their general happiness becomes.

The two main arguments against this are (a) the concept, form, and function of sisyphean absurdism and (b) the concept, form, and function of the hedonic treadmill. I contend that both of these arguments are rooted in misanthropy (the hatred of humanity), which in turn, is a consequence of disconnecting oneself from the unity of the universe, severing one's relationship with Hashem.

Sisyphean Absurdism

The myth of Sisyphus originates from Greek mythology and has been a subject of philosophical contemplation for centuries. It is a tale that embodies the concept of existential absurdity and the eternal struggle of humanity against the inevitability of fate.

Sisyphus was a cunning and deceitful king of Corinth who dared to challenge the gods. One of his most audacious acts was to trick and imprison Thanatos, the personification of death, so that no mortal could die while Thanatos was held captive. This act disrupted the natural order of life and death, causing great chaos among both mortals and gods. In response to Sisyphus's defiance, Zeus, the king of the gods, devised a fitting punishment. He condemned Sisyphus to an eternity of labor in the depths of the underworld. There, Sisyphus was tasked with pushing a massive boulder up a steep hill. However, just as he neared the summit, the boulder would invariably slip from his grasp and roll back down to the bottom, forcing him to begin the task anew, repeating the cycle for eternity.

The myth of Sisyphus has been interpreted in various ways throughout history, but one prevailing interpretation is existentialist in nature, particularly championed by the philosopher Albert Camus. In Camus's essay titled "The Myth of Sisyphus," he explores the idea that life is inherently absurd and devoid of intrinsic meaning, much like Sisyphus's futile task. Despite the seemingly hopeless nature of his predicament, Sisyphus persists in his labor.

Sisyphus's eternal struggle symbolizes the absurdity of human existence. Despite his efforts, he is condemned to an endless cycle of meaningless labor. Similarly, humans often find themselves engaged in repetitive tasks or pursuits that seem futile in the grand scheme of things. Rather than succumbing to despair or nihilism,

Sisyphus's acceptance of his fate can be seen as a form of rebellion. By embracing the absurdity of his existence and finding meaning within the struggle itself, he asserts his autonomy and freedom in the face of an indifferent universe.

Despite the futility of his task, Sisyphus persists in his labor. His resilience in the face of an ultimately meaningless existence underscores the human capacity for perseverance and determination, even in the most challenging circumstances, and, while Sisyphus cannot escape his punishment, he retains the freedom to choose his response to it. In this sense, the myth highlights the significance of personal agency and the ability to find meaning and purpose in one's actions, even in situations beyond one's control.

Overall, the myth of Sisyphus serves as a powerful allegory for the human condition, prompting reflection on the nature of existence, resilience in the face of adversity, and the pursuit of meaning in a seemingly meaningless world.

The Problem With Absurdism

The original myth of Sisyphus conveys the anguish of an eternal punishment, serving as a cautionary tale against disrespecting higher powers. Albert Camus later explored this myth, suggesting that despite the seemingly endless cycle of punishment and suffering, Sisyphus could find happiness through his perseverance. This modern interpretation invites reflection on resilience in the face of adversity. However, Camus' existentialist viewpoint, which posits that life is inherently meaningless, underpins this perspective.

In contrast to existentialist beliefs, Judaism offers a different approach. Rather than embracing the absurdity of existence, Judaism emphasizes the significance of a profound relationship with Hashem (God). Central to Jewish teachings is the notion of performing meaningful actions, even when the reasoning behind them may not be immediately apparent, because they are commanded by Hashem. This emphasis on obedience enhances the bond between individuals and the Divine, instilling a sense of trust in Hashem's wisdom and guidance.

An analogy can be drawn to interpersonal relationships: if someone asks me to perform a seemingly arbitrary task and explains that it is necessary for building trust, my compliance strengthens our bond. Similarly, by following Hashem's commands, even when we may not fully understand their purpose, Jews deepen their connection to the Divine and reinforce their faith. This act of trust strengthens the relationship between individuals and Hashem, fostering a sense of devotion and reliance on Divine guidance within the Jewish community.

The Hedonic Treadmill

The hedonic treadmill is the idea that an individual's level of happiness, after rising or falling in response to positive or negative life events, ultimately tends to move back toward where it was prior to these experiences. It is a psychological phenomenon wherein individuals quickly return to a relatively stable level of happiness or subjective well-being, despite experiencing significant positive or negative events or life changes. This concept suggests that people have a baseline level of happiness, and although they may experience short-term fluctuations in happiness due to external circumstances, they tend to revert to this baseline over time.

The term "hedonic" refers to pleasure or happiness, and the metaphor of a treadmill implies that individuals are constantly striving for happiness but never truly achieving a lasting increase in satisfaction. This phenomenon can be observed across various aspects of life, including income, relationships, material possessions, and even major life events such as marriage, job promotions, or the acquisition of wealth.

One of the key factors driving the hedonic treadmill is adaptation. As humans adapt to new circumstances, the initial boost in happiness that accompanies positive changes tends to diminish over time. Similarly, individuals often adapt to negative circumstances and find ways to cope or adjust, leading to a reduction in the negative impact on their overall well-being. Despite the widespread pursuit of happiness, research suggests that individuals tend to overestimate the long-term impact of positive events and underestimate their resilience in the face of adversity. This cognitive bias can contribute to a continual cycle of seeking happiness through external means, such as material possessions or achievements, only to find that the anticipated satisfaction is short-lived.

Recognizing the tendency to adapt to both positive and negative changes can help individuals manage their expectations and appreciate the transient nature of happiness derived from external sources. Instead of relying solely on external factors for happiness, individuals can cultivate inner qualities such as gratitude, mindfulness, and compassion, which have been shown to contribute to long-term well-being.

Investing in meaningful relationships and engaging in experiences that align with personal values and interests can provide more lasting sources of fulfillment than material possessions or achievements. Regularly practicing gratitude and mindfulness can help individuals savor positive experiences and cultivate a greater sense of contentment with life as it is, rather than constantly striving for more. Additionally, striving for a balanced lifestyle that prioritizes physical health, mental well-being, meaningful connections, and personal growth can contribute to a more sustainable and fulfilling life, rather than chasing fleeting moments of happiness on the hedonic treadmill.

In essence, understanding the hedonic treadmill underscores the importance of cultivating a holistic approach to well-being that encompasses both external circumstances and internal states of mind. By shifting focus from the pursuit of fleeting pleasures to the cultivation of lasting sources of happiness and fulfillment, individuals can transcend the limitations of the hedonic treadmill and lead more fulfilling lives.

The Problem With The Hedonic Treadmill

This concept is flawed because the thought that humans adapt quickly to major changes in life mistakenly asserts that major changes in life are not through one's environment. One's well-being is determined by their nature and nurture. Their genetic disposition may establish their initial hedonic set point, but their environment greatly affects their current hedonic set point. What defines a life change as major or minor is dependent on their environment. Thus, humans do not adapt quickly to major changes in life.

One's general attitude is often dependent on their environment and major life changes change this environment. Without changing their environment, humans generally feel the same after both positive and negative major life changes, but that's because the so-called major life changes were not major enough to change their environment. A wedding may appear like a major life change, but if the pair were already cohabitating and were essentially married in all but name, then that wedding will likely not affect the pair's hedonic set points, meaning that it's not really a major life change for the purposes of the hedonic treadmill.

Duality & Symmetries

The humanity/heavenly interaction, the fundamental duality, gives us symmetries.

Hasidic Judaism emphasizes the interconnectedness of the physical and spiritual realms. According to Hasidic teachings, there exists a profound parallel between the material world and the heavenly realm, with each reflecting and influencing the other in a dynamic interplay. This duality offers deep insights into the nature of existence and the relationship between the finite and the infinite. The physical world, as perceived by the senses, is characterized by tangible objects, material wealth, and temporal experiences. It is governed by natural laws and subject to the passage of time. In contrast, the heavenly world, or spiritual realm, transcends the limitations of the physical and is imbued with Divine energy, cosmic significance, and eternal truths. It is the domain of the soul, where spiritual growth, enlightenment, and connection to the Divine are paramount. Despite their apparent differences, Hasidic Judaism teaches that the physical and spiritual realms are intimately connected, with each influencing and reflecting the other. This connection is manifested in various ways:

Duality

Hasidic teachings emphasize the concept of "Divine immanence," which asserts that God's presence permeates every aspect of creation, from the smallest atom to the vast expanse of the cosmos. Thus, the physical world is not separate from God but rather a manifestation of His Divine energy.

According to Hasidic belief, every object, action, and experience in the physical world has the potential to serve a sacred purpose and elevate the soul. Through acts of kindness, prayer, and observance of mitzvot (commandments), individuals can infuse their mundane existence with spiritual significance and draw closer to God.

Hasidic teachings emphasize the concept of "avodah b'gashmiut," or "service through physicality," which suggests that spiritual growth can be achieved through engagement with the material world. By fulfilling their earthly responsibilities with integrity, humility, and devotion, individuals can refine their character traits, cultivate moral virtues, and deepen their spiritual awareness.

In Hasidic thought, the goal is not to transcend the physical world but rather to harmonize and elevate it through spiritual practice. By integrating spiritual principles into daily life and cultivating mindfulness, individuals can achieve a sense of balance and wholeness that transcends the dichotomy between the physical and spiritual realms.

From the duality of the physical and spiritual worlds, we can glean several symmetries and lessons:

Symmetries

Despite their apparent differences, the physical and spiritual realms are ultimately unified in their source and purpose. Recognizing the interconnectedness of all existence fosters a sense of unity and empathy, promoting harmony and cooperation among many types of individuals and communities.

Hasidic teachings emphasize the importance of embracing both the material and spiritual dimensions of existence. By cultivating a holistic approach to life that integrates body, mind, and soul, individuals can attain a deeper sense of fulfillment and purpose.

The duality of the physical and spiritual realms serves as a reminder of the inherent complexity and paradoxical nature of existence. By transcending dualistic thinking and embracing the synthesis of opposites, individuals can expand their consciousness and attain higher levels of spiritual awareness.

Hasidic Judaism teaches that the Divine Presence can be found in the most ordinary and mundane aspects of life. By cultivating a sense of awe, gratitude, and reverence for the beauty and wonder of creation, individuals can experience profound moments of spiritual connection in everyday moments.

The duality of the physical and spiritual worlds in Hasidic Judaism offers profound insights into the nature of existence and the relationship between the finite and the infinite. By recognizing the interconnectedness of all creation, embracing a holistic approach to life, transcending dualistic thinking, and cultivating a sense of awe and reverence for the Divine, individuals can navigate the complexities of existence with wisdom, grace, and spiritual insight.

Faith-Based Axioms

Remember postulates from the very beginning? Another name for a postulate is an axiom. In mathematics and logic, axioms are used to establish the foundation of a formal system. These axioms are chosen to be simple, consistent, and intuitively true, and from them, other statements or theorems can be derived using logical rules of inference. In the first section, the five postulates of Euclid serve as the axioms upon which the entire system is built.

In philosophy and science, axioms are often used as starting points or presuppositions for developing theories or arguments. These axioms may not be self-evident in the same way as mathematical axioms but are instead accepted based on their plausibility or coherence with other beliefs or observations. Faith-based axioms operate within the realm of religion or spirituality, where beliefs are often grounded in faith rather than empirical evidence or logical deduction. These axioms are typically propositions that are accepted as true based on religious teachings, scripture, personal experiences, or revelation. Unlike mathematical or scientific axioms, faith-based axioms may not be subject to empirical verification or logical demonstration.

The logical workings of faith-based axioms depend on the internal coherence of the belief system in which they are embedded and the acceptance of these axioms by adherents. While faith-based axioms may not be subject to the same standards of empirical or logical verification as mathematical or scientific axioms, they can still provide a framework for understanding the world, guiding ethical behavior, and finding meaning and purpose in life for those who hold them.

The underlying logic within the Jewish understanding of the universe is based on numerous truths. Translating these axioms deepens one's knowledge of the logic fundamental to Judaism, specifically Hasidism. Judaism uses faith-related axioms to create logical Jewish theorems. Since math is logic and logic is math, if it's possible to translate the theorems based on faith-adjacent axioms into mathematical statements, then those theorems must be internally logical.

For example, in Hasidic Judaism, every action one can do, whether that be through the fulfillment of commandments, through speech, or through thought, has the potential to be Divine. Also, humanity has the capability of changing any action's' level of divinity by accepting or not accepting the responsibility. Combining these axioms establishes an understanding of how free will works in Hasidic Judaism - humanity has the free will to change the level of divinity in the physical world through fulfillment of responsibilities that are designed to maximize the level of divinity of the physical world.

The process of working with philosophical axioms has actually furthered the progress of math itself. In trying to solve the cubic ($ax^3 + bx^2 + cx + d$), the only way the study of math progressed was through giving up reality, and embracing the idea of using numbers that are not real - imaginary numbers.

"*Imaginary numbers, discovered as a quirky, intermediate step on the way to solving the cubic, turn out to be fundamental to our description of reality. Only by giving up math's connection to reality could it guide us to a deeper truth about the way the universe works*" (Derek Muller[3]).

Solving the cubic required expanding our understanding of the world to include the potential of negative and imaginary numbers. In trying to put together a logical Jewish theory of everything, we might stumble into a deeper truth about the workings of the universe.

—

[3] From the youtube channel, Veritasium, <https://youtu.be/cUzklzVXJwo?si=X6gAZ2jIjiXHAeMD> 21:56

Underlying Logic

In exploring the underlying logic behind Judaism, we can draw parallels with mathematical structures and principles. Just as mathematics seeks to uncover the underlying patterns and principles governing the universe, Judaism seeks to elucidate the rational foundations underlying its laws and beliefs. One way to conceptualize this is through the lens of axioms and theorems. In mathematics, axioms are the fundamental assumptions upon which a system is built, while theorems are logical conclusions derived from these axioms. Similarly, in Judaism, the Torah serves as the foundational text containing the fundamental principles and commandments (axioms) upon which the entire system of Jewish law and belief is constructed.

Mathematics also employs deductive reasoning to derive new truths from existing ones. Similarly, Jewish legal and philosophical traditions utilize deductive reasoning to interpret and apply the principles laid out in the Torah to new situations and contexts. Furthermore, just as mathematics encompasses various branches such as algebra, geometry, and calculus, Judaism encompasses various areas of study such as Halakha (Jewish law), Aggadah (narrative interpretations), and Jewish philosophy. Each branch offers its own set of principles and methods for understanding and interpreting the underlying logic of Jewish tradition. Moreover, mathematical concepts such as symmetry, proportionality, and harmony can also be applied metaphorically to understand the coherence and balance within Jewish teachings and practices.

By approaching Judaism with a mathematical mindset, we can appreciate its logical structure and systematic approach to understanding the timeless truths and principles embedded within its teachings. Just as mathematics reveals the elegant beauty and order of the universe, Judaism reveals the profound wisdom and depth of insight into the human condition and our relationship with the Divine.

One Talmudic axiom is the **Axiom of Ethical Consistency.** This axiom asserts that mathematical systems should adhere to ethical principles and promote justice, fairness, and compassion. It reflects the Talmudic emphasis on ethical behavior and righteous conduct. Mathematically, this axiom could be expressed as: "In any mathematical system, operations and principles should align with ethical values, promoting fairness, justice, and compassion."

Another one is the **Axiom of Interpretive Flexibility**. Rooted in the Talmudic tradition of multiple interpretations and discussions, this axiom acknowledges the subjectivity inherent in mathematical interpretation and encourages flexibility in understanding mathematical concepts. It can be stated as: "Mathematical truths may be interpreted through various lenses and perspectives, allowing for flexibility in understanding and application."

There is also the **Axiom of Holistic Integration**. Inspired by the Talmudic approach of integrating various sources and ideas, this axiom emphasizes the interconnectedness of mathematical concepts and their integration into a cohesive framework. It can be expressed as: "Mathematical systems should strive for holistic integration, incorporating Jewish concepts and principles into a unified framework that fosters coherence and completeness."

All of these axioms form the set of rules which govern Talmudic logic, but there is one more Judaic axiom worth discussing, and it is much more complex.

Axiom of Divine-Human Action

Humans interact with the Divine through every action.

This leads to understanding of the human ability to accept or reject divinity through their action. Let's explain this through the logic within math. By showing the Judaic understanding of human free will through math, we can better grasp the coherent logic within Judaism.

Given that:

- **A** is an individual's single action in terms of maximizing the Divinity of the physical world of appearances.

- **b** is the total number of human actions.

- **c** is the total number of actions done by everyone else, not the individual.

- **d** is the total number of actions done by an individual.

- **F** is the current level of Divinity within an action.

- **M** is the maximum level of Divinity possible within an action.

- **X** is the difference between the Divinity of the world of ultimate truth and the physical world.

We can derive the following:

$$0 \leq (A^b) - (A^b) \leq 1$$

The difference between the level of Divinity of all humans (A^B) and the level of Divinity of everyone else (A^C) is somewhere between nothingness (0) and perfection (1).

$$(A^b) - (A^c) = A^d$$

Everyone minus everyone else is the same as a single individual.

A = (ΔF / M)
A^d = ((ΔF / M) ^ d)

An individual's average level of Divinity for a single act (A) to the power of the number of acts done by that individual (d) is defined as follows: The current level of Divinity in a single act (F), which humans can change (Δ), divided by the maximum level of Divinity possible in that act (M) gives us the level of divinity as a percentage of perfection. This, raised to the power of the number of actions possible over one's life (d) is equivalent to A^d.

The free will of humanity, the ability to change one's level of Divinity within the human world, can be logically defined as the change (Δ) in the current level of Divinity (F) over the maximum potential (M) of Divinity within that act.

HYPOTHETICALLY: If you were to stop time, since the current level of Divinity would not change for however long time is stopped, you wouldn't need to include the change (Δ). In that scenario, A would equal F over M, and since the current Divinity of an action is never more than the maximum potential, (A) would represent the current level of divinity as a number between 0 and 1. We use the triangle symbol, Delta, to represent an undefined change. So Delta F logically introduces the concept of a constantly-changing F, so it's a constantly changing current level of Divinity. That is a mathematical representation of free will.

$$((\Delta F / M)^{\wedge} d) + X = 1$$

$$(A^{\wedge}d) + X = 1$$

$$1 - (A^{\wedge}d) = X$$

The difference between A^d, which is the same as ($\Delta F / M$)^ d, and perfection is X. In Judaism, the purpose of life is to lower the value of X, thus bridging the gap between the current level of Divinity in the physical world and perfection.

Sacred Geometry

Sacred geometry in Hasidic Judaism is a fascinating concept that combines math, spirituality, and symbolism. Imagine looking at a beautiful piece of artwork or a stunning building and noticing how certain shapes and patterns repeat themselves. These shapes and patterns have special meanings in Hasidic Judaism, connecting the physical world with the spiritual realm. In Hasidic teachings, sacred geometry is often associated with the idea of "sacred proportions" or "Divine symmetry." This means that certain geometric shapes, such as circles, triangles, and squares, are believed to hold deep spiritual significance because they reflect the Divine order and harmony of the universe.

The following explanation of sacred geometry may not be accepted in Hasidism or in Judaism, but this is the clearest explanation of Sacred Geometry I can do.

Tree of Life

An important aspect of sacred geometry in Hasidic Judaism is the concept of the Tree of Life. This mystical symbol is made up of ten interconnected circles, known as the sefirot, which represent different attributes of God and aspects of the human soul. The Tree of Life is believed to serve as a roadmap for spiritual growth and self-discovery, guiding individuals on their journey toward enlightenment and unity with the Divine.

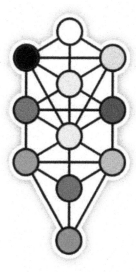

The following list uses "th" to represent the Hebrew character that looks like the character taf. It can be pronounced as "T", "th", or "S" depending on the branch of Judaism. The list also uses "ch" to represent the guttural throat sound of the Hebrew chet.

1. **Kether** is the highest thing that can be perceived by our human consciousness; the maximum potential for anything to come into being, but only the pure potential.

2. **Chochma** is the epitome of wisdom, a boundless energy through which pure creation can take place. It is to the bottom-right of Kether.

3. **Binah** is located at the same level as Chochma. It's the stable understanding through which form can take place. Chochma and Binah combine together in creation.

4. **Chesed** is just below Chochma. It is the mercy and loving kindness; the connection in the universe appearing through love and peace.

5. **Geburah** is just below Bina and mirrors Chesed. It is the strength that carries out the rules of the universe, the laws of everything, through order and function. Combined together, Geburah and Chesed allow for the creation and application of the rules of the universe.

6. **Tifareth** connects to every other sefira. It's the beauty and connectedness of everything. It's the bridge between the previously mentioned formless forces and the forces of form.

7. **Netzach** is the victory over obstacles. It's just below Chesed, and is the Hasidic representation of qualia.

8. **Hod** is the mirror of Netzach just below Geburah. It's our thoughts and identity. Combined together, they represent the human dichotomy of animal and Hashem.

9. **Yesod** connects Netzach and Hod. It's how the Divine emanations engage with physical reality.

10. **Malkuth** is the representation of the four fundamental elements of the physical world.

11. The sefira located just beneath Kether, called **Da'at** is a bit more complicated than the rest. The Tree of Life always has ten sefirot, and Da'at is commonly referred to as all ten united as one, but when it is counted within the 10, Kether is removed from the count because Hashem's infinity, Kether, cannot be understood by humans. Da'at represents memory and concentration, relying upon the recognition of Chochma and Bina. The trifecta of Chocha, Bina, and Da'at is commonly combined together to form the Hasidic denomination of ChaBaD, later spread around the world as Chabad-Lubavitch.

Magen David

One of the most well-known symbols in Judaism as a whole is the Star of David, which is formed by two interlocking triangles. Each triangle represents different aspects of the Divine – one pointing upwards toward the heavens, symbolizing the connection to Hashem, and the other pointing downwards toward the earth, symbolizing the manifestation of God's presence in the physical world. The Star of David is often seen as a symbol of protection and unity, reminding believers of their connection to the Divine and to each other.

Overall, sacred geometry in Hasidic Judaism is a way of understanding and experiencing the Divine presence in the world. By exploring the meanings and symbolism behind geometric shapes and patterns, believers can deepen their connection to Hashem and gain insight into the mysteries of the universe.

A Logical Conclusion

The Nambu-Goto and Polyakov actions are mathematical descriptions used in the study of String Theory to describe how the fundamental strings move through spacetime. Sacred geometry in Judaism involves geometric shapes and patterns that are considered to have spiritual significance. One of the most famous geometric patterns in Judaism is the Star of David, which is formed by the intersection of two equilateral triangles.

While it might seem like a stretch to connect these concepts, there are significant parallels between these two understandings.

One connection is found in the concept of harmony and the idea that fundamental principles govern both the physical universe and spiritual realms. In sacred geometry, certain shapes are believed to represent underlying principles of creation and existence. Similarly, in String Theory, the behavior of strings is governed by mathematical principles encoded in the universal geometry explained by the Nambu-Goto and Polyakov actions. Both sacred geometry and String Theory deal with the idea of hidden structures underlying reality. In sacred geometry, there's often an emphasis on uncovering deeper meanings and patterns within geometric shapes. In String Theory, the search for a unified theory of fundamental forces involves uncovering hidden dimensions and symmetries. The fundamentals of String Theory require the understanding that everything in the universe is a product of the geometry encoded within the fabric of the universe.

It's impossible to imagine a world where Pi doesn't describe the ratio between the circle's circumference and its diameter. It seems as if logic is built into the geometry of the universe, and if so, then by (a) studying the variety in understandings of universal geometry, and (b) not dismissing an understanding simply because it's not yet mathematically proven, we can (c) derive a theory of everything that includes Jewish thought.

Religion is our immovable object, near ultimate truth, through which faith-based understandings of existence originate, and sets the background on which a true theory of everything must manifest.

—

XOOT

These two theories of everything are the same.

From the simple, conceptual parallels, we can understand the fascinating overlap. Correlation does not necessarily mean causation, but in this case, (a) one does not affect the other. They are both the same. And (b) studying the correlation is a necessary first step to understand the underlying fundamental connection.

—

The Qualia Paradox

What is Qualia?

That's a tough question to answer; to simply define it is to misunderstand. Qualia is experience, how we feel, and who we truly are. Qualia is you experiencing color, sight, sound, taste, touch, etc. Qualia is not the wavelength of light that we define as yellow. It's our experience seeing the color yellow.

There is no current way to understand qualia objectively, and due to its subjective nature, to understand another person's qualia, one must share the exact same experience, including the exact same stimulation. For example, given that you can see the color yellow, by showing a picture of something yellow to another non-blind person, you and this person now fully understand that experience of seeing that color in that shade at that time. Through this method, the experience was shared, and therefore, understood.

Now, what if you were to attempt to share the experience of seeing the color yellow with someone who cannot see. It cannot be done. Some may try to compare seeing the color yellow with a sharable experience of feeling somewhat hot, but that is not the same. If, however, two colorblind people were to explain the shareable experience of not seeing a color, that experience translates well, quickly becoming recognition and true connection - consider that most individuals unable to see the color green experience green as off-white.

Now, apply this current lack of objective understandability to consciousness. The problem of trying to understand how and why humans have qualia experiences and consciousness is fittingly called *the Hard Problem of Consciousness*. It's hard, because, scientifically, we don't even have a beginning of a beginning of a clue as to how it works, and the requirement for the scientific solution is a great leap tantamount to Newton's assertion that the rules that exist on Earth exist everywhere.

How our brains analyze the outside world and turn it into experience is the key question of the Hard Problem, and every possible solution could be correct, but the best use of that problem is to lead us into the real questions: why do we, as humans, have this awareness, is it connected to why we have qualia, and why does qualia supersede written language - the one thing that makes us uniquely human? Attempting to answer one of these questions brings out several more, like trying to solve a Sudoku puzzle with only a few boxes filled. In our Sudoku puzzle metaphor, only one box is pre-filled, representing the only thing we know for absolute certainty, that we have a fundamental awareness.

You cannot prove that qualia and consciousness exist, yet you cannot be more certain of anything else. This is what I define as the

Qualia Paradox, and it's what makes the studies of both qualia and consciousness continuously fascinating.

Metaphysical solutions to the Qualia Paradox are many in number, but there is no universally agreed-upon answer - if a universal answer can even be knowable. Thus, the most logical solution is whichever one gives you the most comfort, at least until science discovers how we are meat that knows we're meat.

This is solutional fluidity, and in times of solutional fluidity, it may be tempting to view all possibilities as completely isolated.

This cannot coexist with the fact that when compiling potential answers to possibly impossible questions, very often understandings meld into a universal theory. These possibilities/understandings/potential answers are neither entirely isolated nor entirely designed to fit together, but if we understand that there is a universal theory of everything, then not all solutions have merit. Humans have a tendency to find the solution that best allows one to think inquisitively and to merit one's personal antagonists with the right to be heard, but not the right to be right.

I contend that the metaphysical solution to the Qualia Paradox within Judaism works incredibly well with String Theory, the most well-developed current scientific explanation of everything. When it comes to the universe, science answers *how*, Judaism answers *why*; but the process of answering *why* should logically include *how*.

Xoot Assertion

String Theory, the most complicated and dynamic topic in physics, the pinnacle of human scientific achievement, and the closest science has come to a theory of everything, is identical to Jewish thought. The current inability to reconcile gravity with the standard model of particle physics is one of the greatest scientific challenges, and String Theory solves this by asserting that there are microscopic strings that create everything through their vibrations and movements. By studying how these strings vibrate and move, we can understand the fundamental nature of our universe. Surprisingly enough, Judaism, through the works of Hassidic literature, asserts the exact same thing. There are, according to Hassidic understanding, invisible strings that are so fundamentally embedded in the universe that the work of creation is done through their movement.

If the similarities ended there, most would view this as a fascinating, but otherwise unimportant, coincidence. Fortunately, this is only the beginning. Both broad and specific aspects of String Theory parallel identically to Hassidic work, including, but not limited to, the notion of inherent motion, the underlying unity & oneness, the logical resolution of paradoxes, and the number and nature of dimensions beyond our own. Unfortunately, very few individuals are intricately familiar with both topics, even though both have the same understanding of the universe.

Xoot attempts to explain both topics in such a way that someone without a high-level mathematical understanding and/or without years of Jewish study can understand the nature and reasoning behind why and how both are intrinsically connected. One must understand both deep enough to see that the major concepts, minor concepts, and even specifics eerily match.

The religious world and the scientific world generally have differences in the questions they answer about the universe: science answers how, religion answers why, but the modern scientific understanding of the world is usually focused on treating religious claims as insincere babbling. It's tough to argue against that by saying that X religion is right, because that argument requires that one agrees with the scientific treatment of religious claims when it comes to over 99% of world religions but should treat exactly one religion differently despite the similarities between that religion's claim and the 99%. However, the Jewish claims are unique in many valid ways, such as Divine revelation of the entire nation which is a notoriously difficult claim to uphold - if one person in the nation disagreed, the claim would falter; and let's not forget that String Theory ventures into many realms of abstract concepts without empirical evidence, seemingly operating as an unscientific approach in the modern era.

Scientific reasoning, even through a global scientific consensus, is incorrect often. I'm not claiming that the Earth is flat, nor am I denying the empirical evidence provided by modern science, but I am stating that the modern way of seeing the world scientifically evolves as new technology arises. Science consistently proves itself wrong and that's OK. Psychology used to be about compression and diversion of pressure because the pinnacle of technology at the time was the steam engine. A common way of thinking of the world scientifically now is through the lens of computation and simulation because the pinnacle of technology in our modern world is computing. As we move into the era of Artificial Intelligence, science and religion may finally agree that there is a higher intelligence controlling everything but disagree on our relationship with it or Him.

Agree or Disagree

There are two understandings that one forms after reading the previous assertion: one disagrees or one agrees.

If you disagree that String Theory and Jewish understanding are, at least, somewhat connected, then skip to the next section, as it indicates the many parallels between the two main topics. Otherwise, continue below.

The near-infinite amount of parallels between String Theory and Jewish understanding illuminates a significant problem. If the surface level indicates that String Theory and Jewish understandings are identical, why study any deeper than that? Why must I learn in-depth instead of simply agreeing that these understandings of the universe are identical? The answer can best be explained through the following analogy.

Jake and Tai are brilliant experts in their fields, but speak completely different languages. They both have perfect recall and have added large amounts of knowledge in their respective fields. They have never met and know nothing about one another, but when a journalist asked them how they think the universe works, they both independently give the exact same answer. At first, nobody notices the similarity in their answers, but when each answer is translated in the other respective language, everyone assumes it to have been a weird coincidence or mistranslation. Later, another journalist asked each one of them to expound on their previous answers. The more detailed answers are translated, and miraculously, each detail of the two more-detailed answers are, point-for-point, identical. Eventually, it becomes clear to both Jake and Tai that there must be an objective understanding of the universe that encompasses both Jake's field and Tai's field. They meet up, learn each other's language, and, through many years of shared research and study, they successfully prove their ultimate theory of everything.

Simply agreeing that String Theory and Jewish understanding are identical is cutting off this analogy just as everyone assumes the simple answers' similarity is just a coincidence. Without proving it or going into detail, your explanation of what you learned from this book will be quickly disregarded as a weird coincidence. If you prove it or go into detail, this may entice some extremely intelligent experts in one of these fields of understanding to meet with some extremely intelligent experts in the other field of understanding. Hopefully, these leading experts can form a shared drive to derive the ultimate theory of everything, or at least spend time understanding each other through shared research and study. Right now, the fields of Orthodox Jewish understanding and high-level mathematical-based modern physics are essentially speaking two different languages, preventing any knowledge from reaching the other field through a thick language barrier. I encourage you to learn as much as you can about both fields, especially if you want to be part of the derivation process of the ultimate theory of everything.

The following are essays that introduce parallels between String Theory and Jewish understanding organized into three chapters: Aspect-based, Logic-based, and Modernity-based. If, by reading the second and third sections of this book, you noticed the inherent connection, the following essays may be redundant and I will see you in the next non-redundant chapter, The Superiority of Jewish Rationality, which is the first of a much larger group of chapters designed to translate the logic within Jewish work into the language of String Theory in a natural and earned manner.

—

Parallels

Aspects

It's important to clarify from the outset that String Theory, a complex and mathematically intricate framework aiming to unify fundamental forces and explain the nature of the universe at the quantum level, is a product of modern theoretical physics. Its origins lie within the realm of scientific inquiry, particularly in the efforts of physicists to reconcile quantum mechanics and general relativity. However, some intriguing parallels can be drawn between certain aspects of String Theory and concepts found in mystical or philosophical traditions, including elements of Hassidic Judaism. While these connections are largely speculative and metaphorical rather than direct influences, exploring them can offer insights into the interdisciplinary nature of human thought and the ways in which diverse ideas intersect and inform one another.

At its core, String Theory posits that the fundamental building blocks of the universe are not point-like particles but rather tiny, vibrating strings. These strings oscillate at different frequencies, giving rise to the diverse particles and forces observed in nature. This concept of a fundamental substrate underlying reality bears some resemblance to the notion of the Divine emanations or sefirot in Hassidic Kabbalah. In Hassidic thought, the sefirot are ten attributes through which the Divine interacts with and manifests in the world. Each sefirah represents a different aspect of God's essence, and the interactions between them give rise to the complexity and diversity of creation. The mathematical formalism of String Theory and the framework of Judaism in general share a common theme of underlying unity giving rise to multiplicity.

Hassidic Judaism emphasizes the interconnectedness of all aspects of existence and the notion of everything being imbued with divine sparks or energy. This holistic perspective resonates with the idea in String Theory that all particles and forces arise from the vibrational modes of the fundamental strings, suggesting a fundamental unity underlying the apparent diversity of the physical world.

Both String Theory and Hassidic thought grapple with questions of transcendence and the limits of human understanding. String Theory ventures into realms of higher dimensions and abstract mathematical spaces beyond direct empirical observation, much like mystical explorations of the Divine realm in Kabbalistic traditions. String Theory is firmly rooted in mathematical rigor, experimental evidence, and the scientific method, whereas Hassidic Kabbalah is a spiritual and theological tradition based on faith, revelation, and interpretation of sacred texts, yet the unusually common universal understanding must deal with the limits of human understanding.

While String Theory and Hassidic Judaism occupy vastly different intellectual domains, they share some intriguing conceptual resonances. Exploring these parallels can enrich our understanding of both scientific and spiritual inquiries into the nature of reality, highlighting the diverse ways in which human cultures and traditions seek to make sense of the universe. Ultimately, while String Theory may not be fundamentally rooted in Hassidic Judaism, the intersections between these disparate realms offer fertile ground for interdisciplinary dialogue and exploration.

Modernity

Modern physics attempts to scientifically reconcile subjects present in Hasidism. This has led to a new, deeper understanding of the world.

At its core, Hassidic philosophy offers a unique perspective on the universe, one that resonates deeply with the principles of modern physics. Just as physicists seek to uncover the fundamental laws that govern the cosmos, Hassidic thinkers delve into the mysteries of existence, probing the underlying unity that binds together the disparate elements of creation. Central to Hassidic philosophy is the concept of Tzimtzum, a notion that resonates strongly with the principles of quantum mechanics. Tzimtzum posits a Divine contraction or concealment, akin to the collapse of a quantum wave function, through which the Infinite Creator creates a space for finite existence to emerge. This concept offers a profound insight into the dynamic interplay between the transcendent and the immanent, echoing the wave-particle duality inherent in quantum phenomena.

Hassidic philosophy offers a holistic view of reality, emphasizing the interconnectedness of all things—a perspective that finds resonance in the principles of systems theory and complexity science. Just as physicists study the emergent properties that arise from the interactions of elementary particles, Hassidic thinkers contemplate the intricate web of relationships that define the human experience, recognizing the interconnected nature of body, mind, and soul.

Hassidic philosophy delves into the nature of consciousness and the role of the observer—a theme that parallels the insights of quantum mechanics. Just as physicists grapple with the enigmatic nature of observation and its impact on the behavior of quantum systems, Hassidic thinkers explore the transformative power of spiritual awareness, recognizing the profound influence of consciousness on the fabric of reality.

General Logic

Comparing the logic found in Jewish works like the Talmud and Torah with the mathematical logic found in String Theory reveals intriguing parallels and contrasts between these two seemingly disparate systems of thought. While one is rooted in religious tradition and the other in scientific inquiry, both involve rigorous frameworks for understanding the world and probing the nature of reality.

In Jewish texts such as the Talmud, scholars engage in intricate analysis and interpretation of sacred texts to derive legal, ethical, and philosophical insights. This process involves careful examination of the text, consideration of various commentaries and interpretations, and application of logical reasoning to resolve apparent contradictions or ambiguities. Similarly, in String Theory, physicists employ mathematical logic to interpret and analyze the equations and principles underlying the theory. They engage in complex calculations, theoretical modeling, and conceptual frameworks to derive predictions about the behavior of fundamental particles and forces.

Jewish legal reasoning often involves hierarchical structures of principles, where broader principles serve as the basis for more specific rulings or interpretations. Scholars navigate this hierarchy to apply overarching ethical or legal principles to specific cases. In String Theory, mathematical logic also operates within a hierarchical framework, where fundamental principles such as symmetry, duality, and quantum mechanics serve as the basis for deriving more specific results and predictions. Physicists navigate this hierarchy to understand how the fundamental principles of the theory manifest in observable phenomena.

Both Jewish texts and String Theory confront paradoxes and apparent contradictions. In the Talmud, for example, scholars use logical reasoning and textual analysis to resolve conflicting statements or principles. This often involves reconciling different interpretations or synthesizing seemingly opposing viewpoints. In String Theory, physicists encounter paradoxes such as the black hole information paradox or the apparent conflict between general relativity and quantum mechanics. They employ mathematical logic and theoretical insights to propose resolutions to these paradoxes, often leading to new theoretical frameworks or conceptual breakthroughs.

Jewish texts frequently use metaphorical language and conceptual frameworks to convey abstract concepts or spiritual insights. Analogies, parables, and allegories are employed to help readers grasp complex theological or ethical ideas. Similarly, in String Theory, physicists often use conceptual frameworks and metaphors to elucidate abstract mathematical concepts or theoretical constructs. Analogies drawn from everyday experiences or familiar physical phenomena help communicate the essence of complex ideas such as extra dimensions or quantum entanglement.

While there may be seemingly significant differences between the logic found in Jewish works and the mathematical logic of String Theory, exploring these parallels highlights the ways in which human intellect seeks to make sense of the world. Whether through religious interpretation or scientific inquiry, the quest for understanding and meaning remains a fundamental aspect of human culture and civilization.

In both of these attempted theories of everything within one's respective field, it would be logically coherent that the ways in which humans make sense of the world have significant overlap *IF* these theories of everything were really different angles of one larger theory of everything.

Specific Examples

Easy Three & Bad Guy

The parallels between Judaism's concept of the four fundamental forces of the physical world and the four fundamental forces of String Theory offer a fascinating lens through which to explore the interconnectedness of spirituality and science. In Judaism, the concepts of Atzilut, Bria, Yetzira, and Asi'a align strikingly with the four major forces of the universe: electromagnetism, strong nuclear force, weak nuclear force, and gravity.

Atzilut, the highest level in Jewish mysticism, can be likened to gravity in String Theory. Gravity, the force responsible for the attraction between objects with mass, operates at the largest scales in the universe, governing the motion of planets, stars, and galaxies. Similarly, Atzilut represents the Divine force that permeates and governs all existence, exerting its influence over the entire cosmos.

Bria, the second level, corresponds to electromagnetism. Electromagnetism is a fundamental force that manifests as both electric and magnetic fields, governing the behavior of charged particles and electromagnetic waves. In Jewish mysticism, Bria represents the realm where the Divine energy begins to manifest in distinct forms, much like electromagnetism manifests in various phenomena such as light, electricity, and magnetism.

Yetzira, the third level, finds its parallel in the strong and weak nuclear forces of String Theory. The strong nuclear force binds protons and neutrons together within atomic nuclei, while the weak nuclear force is responsible for certain types of radioactive decay. Similarly, Yetzira symbolizes the realm where divine energy shapes and structures the building blocks of creation, binding them together in intricate patterns.

In the story of hail in Shemot, we see a phenomenon that seemingly defies the laws of physics, akin to how the strong force behaves in contrast to electromagnetism. Similarly, a small amount of light pushes away darkness, where a previously neutral entity transforms into a positive force, driving out negativity, akin to how the weak force behaves. The neutron, lacking agency in this transformation, isn't the most dominant force in nature; it's weak relative to the other forces of the physical world.

Finally, **Asi'a**, the lowest level, stands apart from the others, much like gravity stands apart from the other fundamental forces. While electromagnetism, the strong nuclear force, and the weak nuclear force all operate within the physical world, Asi'a represents a higher level of existence that transcends direct interaction with our reality. This concept aligns with the elusive nature of gravity, which, while influencing the entire universe, is not as readily observable or easily understood as the other forces.

Identical Treatment

Thesis: Understandings of the universe that have strong connections between their parts are treated the same as understandings that have weak connections between their parts.

The thesis above underscores the fundamental principle of interconnectedness in both metaphysics and the relationship between Judaism and String Theory. It highlights that the strength of connections within a conceptual framework is not necessarily indicative of its validity or significance. Instead, it emphasizes the importance of recognizing and exploring the intricate relationships between different aspects of understanding.

This invites us to consider how the interconnectedness of concepts within each framework contributes to their overall coherence and relevance. Judaism, with its rich metaphysical traditions, emphasizes the interconnectedness of all aspects of existence, from the Divine realms to the material world. Similarly, String Theory posits that the universe is composed of vibrating strings whose interactions give rise to all observable phenomena, highlighting the interconnected nature of physical reality.

Both Judaism and String Theory recognize that the strength of connections between different components of understanding varies. In Judaism, concepts such as the Sephirot—the Divine emanations—and the Four Worlds illustrate different levels of connection between spiritual realms and the material world. Similarly, in String Theory, the strength of interactions between fundamental particles and forces determines the properties and behavior of matter and energy.

However, the thesis suggests that the significance of these connections transcends their strength. Whether the connections within a framework are strong or weak does not diminish their importance in shaping our understanding of the universe. In fact, it is often the exploration of weaker connections that leads to breakthroughs in knowledge and new avenues of inquiry. It challenges us to approach the study of metaphysics and scientific theories with an open mind, recognizing that diverse perspectives and levels of interconnectedness can enrich our understanding of the cosmos. Just as Judaism offers insights into the spiritual dimensions of existence, String Theory provides a framework for understanding the underlying structure of the universe. By acknowledging the parallels and intersections between these two realms of inquiry, we can cultivate a deeper appreciation for the interconnected nature of reality.

For example, the whole idea of having a machloket, a reasoned argument, is to deduce a logical conclusion within Judaism. There are things that are directly from Torah, and things that are best left to debate and logical reasoning. Based on the parameters and the information, we can derive logical inconsistencies, and we treat the process of discovering the hidden truth through logical analysis in the exact same manner as we treat the process of gleaning a simplistic understanding of the Torah. In Judaism, one should follow both rabbinical-based Jewish laws and biblical-based Jewish laws, indicating that one should treat the process and results of rigorous debates in the same manner as the relatively simplistic commandments within the Torah.

Extra Dimensions

Central to the mystical teachings of Hasidic Judaism is the concept of the Sefirot, emanations through which the Divine interacts with and manifests in the world. The Sefirot represent the attributes or qualities through which God reveals Himself and sustains creation. These attributes are often depicted as ten interconnected spheres, each representing a different aspect of the Divine essence. From the primordial source of Keter (Crown) to the manifest kingdom of Malchut (Kingship), the Sefirot form a complex network of divine energies that underpin the spiritual architecture of creation.

In the realm of theoretical physics, String Theory posits that the fundamental building blocks of the universe are not point-like particles but rather tiny, vibrating strings. One of the most intriguing aspects of String Theory is its proposal of extra spatial dimensions beyond the familiar three of length, width, and height, which are essential for the consistency of the theory. While the theory originally posited ten dimensions (nine spatial dimensions plus time), later developments such as M-theory extended this to twenty-six dimensions in certain formulations, providing a framework to reconcile disparate approaches in theoretical physics.

The striking alignment between the ten Sefirot of Hasidic Judaism and the proposed dimensions of String Theory invites deeper contemplation. Both systems offer insights into the underlying structure of reality, albeit from different perspectives. The Sefirot, as divine emanations, represent the unfolding of divine attributes within creation, while the dimensions of String Theory provide a framework for understanding the fundamental fabric of the universe. At first glance, it may seem coincidental that both systems converge on the numbers ten and twenty-six. However, a closer examination reveals deeper connections. In Hasidic thought, the ten Sefirot are not merely arbitrary divisions but represent fundamental aspects of divine revelation and creative energy. Similarly, the dimensions of String Theory are not random but are intricately linked to the mathematical consistency and coherence of the theory.

The alignment between Hasidic Judaism's Sefirot and String Theory's dimensions raises intriguing questions about the nature of reality and the relationship between the spiritual and physical realms. Could there be deeper metaphysical principles underlying both systems, hinting at a profound unity in the fabric of existence, and what insights might this convergence offer into the nature of consciousness, creation, and the ultimate meaning of existence?

Moreso, the parallels between these seemingly disparate disciplines invite interdisciplinary dialogue and exploration. By bridging the gap between religious mysticism and theoretical physics, we may uncover new avenues for understanding the nature of reality and our place within it. This convergence challenges us to expand our perspectives and embrace the richness of diverse intellectual traditions in our quest for truth and understanding.

Overall, the alignment between Hasidic Judaism's ten Sefirot and String Theory's dimensions offers a fascinating glimpse into the interconnectedness of seemingly unrelated realms of knowledge. While rooted in distinct traditions and methodologies, both systems converge on fundamental principles that illuminate the nature of reality in profound ways. As we continue to explore the mysteries of the cosmos and the depths of spiritual wisdom, may we remain open to the possibility of unexpected connections that enrich our understanding and deepen our appreciation of the universe in all its complexity.

Universal Unity

At its core, String Theory suggests that everything in the universe is interconnected through these vibrating strings, creating a unified fabric of reality. Similarly, Modern Orthodox Judaism teaches the concept of universal unity within the Jewish people and their relationship with Hashem. Central to this belief is the idea that all Jews are bound together by a common heritage and destiny, regardless of their individual differences. This unity is expressed through shared rituals, prayers, and values that unite Jews across diverse backgrounds and experiences. Modern Orthodox Judaism, much like other denominations of Judaism, emphasizes the unity of all aspects of Jewish life, including the spiritual, ethical, and communal dimensions. Just as String Theory posits that all particles and forces are interconnected through vibrating strings, Modern Orthodox Judaism teaches that all aspects of Jewish life are interconnected through a shared spiritual essence, and can be studied through the scientific process.

Both String Theory and Modern Orthodox Judaism suggest that this universal unity extends beyond the Jewish people or the physical universe to encompass all of existence. In String Theory, the interconnectedness of vibrating strings implies a fundamental unity that transcends individual particles or forces. Similarly, in Modern Orthodox Judaism, the unity of the Jewish people is seen as part of a larger cosmic unity that encompasses all of creation.

Both concepts emphasize the interconnectedness of all things, whether through vibrating strings in String Theory or through the shared heritage and destiny of the Jewish people. By recognizing this unity, we gain a deeper understanding of the underlying fabric of reality and our place within it.

The Superiority of Jewish Rationality

Throughout this book, it may appear that I am trying to prove that Judaism, specifically Hasidism, is the only correct religion. It may be, but I am not trying to prove that. More often than not, that type of "proof" that one religion or denomination is superior is used as justification for inevitable persecution of those who choose to not follow that religion or denomination. Throughout all of Jewish history, Jews generally want to be left alone to their communities, and it would be foolish to not grant others that same ideological privacy. When I discuss the superiority of Jewish rationality, I focus on the rationality, that the logic, by use of philosophical axioms, is internally consistent. Some religions do not have internally consistent logic, and that's OK, but in the act of defending the allegation that Judaism has ties to String Theory, one must understand how Judaism remains internally logically consistent.

That being said, I subscribe to the Modern Orthodox denomination, and not stating such would be disingenuous to my point. I am certainly biased and my logic may be flawed, but the goal of this text is not to convince you that Judaism is correct. Rather, the goal is to shine a light on the real possibility that there may be something more than just a coincidental alignment between Jewish mysticism and the fundamentals underlying the scientific theory of everything; that through understanding the seemingly least-scientific parts of human existential explanation, maybe in the future, someone could derive a theory of everything that accurately merges science and religion - a theory of truly everything. The point of this section is to explain, through logical reasoning, that even the least-scientific denomination within Judaism is internally consistent.

Throughout human history, religions have provided frameworks for understanding the mysteries of existence, offering explanations for the fundamental questions of life. Among these, Judaism stands out not only for its rich cultural heritage and historical significance but also for the logical coherence of its principles and teachings. By examining the logical foundations of Judaism, we can appreciate its rational approach to spirituality and gain insights into why it may be considered more logical than other religions.

The Importance of Critical Thinking

First and foremost, Judaism emphasizes the importance of rational inquiry and critical thinking. From the Talmudic tradition of rigorous debate and analysis to the philosophical insights of figures like Maimonides, Jewish thought has a long history of intellectual engagement with complex questions.

Unlike some other religions that discourage questioning or skepticism, Judaism encourages inquiry and invites adherents to wrestle with profound theological and ethical issues. Judaism places a strong emphasis on ethical behavior and justice, rooted in logical principles of fairness and compassion, encompassed in the concept of tikkun olam, or repairing the world, which underscores the belief that individuals have a moral responsibility to act in ways that promote the well-being of society and alleviate suffering. This ethical imperative aligns with basic principles of logical reasoning, recognizing the inherent value of empathy, cooperation, and justice. Additionally, Judaism's monotheistic theology offers a logically coherent framework for understanding the nature of the Divine.

Consistent With Occam's Razor

The concept of one God, as articulated in the Shema prayer, reflects a unity and simplicity that is consistent with Occam's razor, the principle that simpler explanations are generally preferable to more complex ones. Unlike polytheistic religions with multiple deities and conflicting mythologies, Judaism's monotheism provides a clear and concise understanding of the Divine. In addition, Judaism's emphasis on textual study and interpretation fosters a culture of intellectual engagement and lifelong learning. The study of sacred texts such as the Torah and Talmud requires careful analysis, logical reasoning, and interpretation, encouraging adherents to develop critical thinking skills and engage with complex ideas. This intellectual rigor distinguishes Judaism as a religion that values intellectual honesty and the pursuit of truth.

Historical Resilience & Adaptability

Furthermore, Judaism's historical resilience and adaptability demonstrate its capacity to evolve in response to changing circumstances while maintaining its core principles. From the Babylonian exile to the challenges of modernity, Judaism has demonstrated an ability to reinterpret its traditions and teachings in ways that are relevant to contemporary concerns. This flexibility reflects a logical approach to religion, recognizing the need for adaptation and innovation while preserving the integrity of foundational beliefs. In conclusion, Judaism's logical coherence, intellectual rigor, ethical values, and adaptability distinguish it as a uniquely rational religion. While other religions may offer different perspectives on the Divine and the human experience, Judaism's emphasis on critical thinking, ethical behavior, and logical reasoning sets it apart as a faith that resonates with the rational mind. By embracing the principles of Judaism, individuals can find meaning, purpose, and spiritual fulfillment within a framework that is both intellectually satisfying and morally compelling.

The Science of Spirituality

Throughout history, humanity has sought to understand the universe by drawing parallels with the most advanced technological achievements of the time. From the early days of psychology likened to the operation of steam engines to the contemporary fascination with the universe as a simulation governed by computational rules, the tendency to use the latest technology as a descriptor for the cosmos persists. However, this practice is fraught with logical fallacies and limitations.

Psychology used to be about compression and diversion of pressure because the pinnacle of technology at the time was the steam engine. Nowadays, it's common to think of the brain as one complicated computer, and the universe as a simulation. The transition from viewing psychology through the lens of steam engines to conceptualizing the universe as a simulated reality reflects the influence of technological paradigms on our understanding of the world. This new perspective has gained traction in scientific discourse through theories like the simulation hypothesis.

Yet, attributing characteristics of computers to the universe oversimplifies both of their complexities and anthropomorphizes phenomena beyond our comprehension. The analogy between the universe and a simulation is inherently temporary and subject to the limitations of human innovation and understanding. What is considered cutting-edge today may be obsolete tomorrow as new discoveries and advancements emerge.

I fully believe that through the rise of AI, humanity will transition into thinking about the scientific implication of an intelligent creator. The transition from viewing the universe as a simulation to positing the existence of an intelligent creator could be a sign that science is catching up with religion; or that the comparison of the universe to modern technology is inherently flawed. Just as steam engines gave way to computers, so too might the simulation hypothesis yield to alternative perspectives as our knowledge evolves, especially as AI challenges our understanding of intelligence and consciousness.

The Fallacy of Comparison is real. The universe is a complex and multifaceted entity that defies simplistic categorization in terms of human-made inventions. Instead of clinging to the latest technological trends, we must approach the study of the cosmos with an openness to varied perspectives, recognizing that our understanding is always evolving and subject to revision.

Now, let's discuss the universe's origin story through the fusion of scientific consensus and Judaism.

Tzimtzum

The concept of Tzimtzum introduces the idea that before creation, this Divine presence was so overwhelming and all-encompassing that there was no room for anything else to exist. In a sense, it's like a stage with a blindingly bright spotlight; everything else is overshadowed and invisible. This sounds an awful lot like the scientific consensus understanding of the origin of our universe; that, through scientific analysis of space expansion, we agree that there was an origin to our universe, and, through powerful telescopes analyzing the visible and invisible aura of the universe, we agree that the universe had a level of brightness [so dense that not even light could travel at its maximum speed] and is now darker after a transformation.

Sacred Geometry

The following argument is internally logical, but may be rooted in philosophical axioms with which one may not agree. In that case, I recommend to follow one of Aristotle's teachings, where he stated that the sign of intelligence is when one can entertain an idea without accepting it wholeheartedly.

Metatron is an angel in the three main monotheistic religions: Judaism, Christianity, and Islam. His name is mentioned a few times in the Talmud, Aggadah, and some Kabbalistic texts. Attributed to him is what's known as Metatron's Cube, through which one can derive all shapes within the geometry of our three-dimensional world. To understand Metatron's Cube, one must first understand what's known as the Genesis Pattern, then the Fruit of Life.

Six circles interlocking around a seventh circle is, in many cultures, considered The Genesis Pattern, a holy union of creation. If the circles are the same size, the ratio of six-to-one seems embedded in logic itself. Through this, there is an argument to be made that within the geometry of our world, the geometric pattern of six-to-one is so fundamental that it must be intentional Divine will. One can easily derive an explanation through which the six days of creation   match   with   fundamental   geometry.

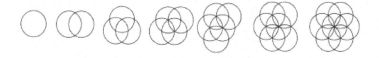

There are seven shapes above. We do not begin with the first shape, as it represents perfection manifested in the physical three-dimensional world.

Day one establishes a division between light and dark. This contains an incredible amount of knowledge about width, proportion, and depth, as well as some information about light itself. The act of Hashem's "movement" on the first day can be interpreted as the spirit of creation physically moving to the edge of what had been created, then creating light. Why not mention that there was some element of creation prior to the first day? Well, the act of moving to then create light both establishes the creation of light and the creation of relative movement. A line prior to this statement in the Torah would be redundant, and within Judaism, there are no redundancies, thus, the line need not be written.

Each successive day, through each successive circle, adds exponentially more information.

If we expand this pattern by adding one more layer of circles, we end up with the Seed of Life.

This is used as the geometric origin of the Kabbalistic Tree of Life. Adding one more layer of circles allows us to easily visualize how that might work.

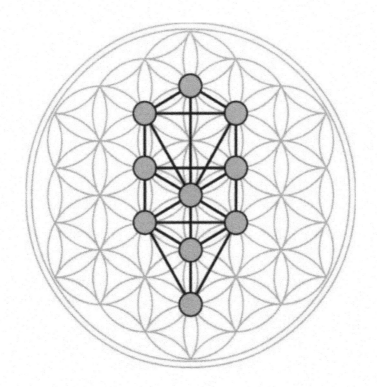

Many cultures and civilizations throughout history used this background pattern, but would rarely move beyond it. Expanding this even further allows us to notice a particular pattern that is fundamental to three-dimensional geometry.

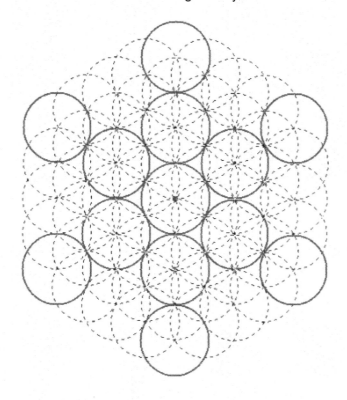

This pattern in red is called the Fruit of Life, sprouted from the Seed of Life, and originating from the creation of everything.

If we move away from circles and connect the centers of each one of these red circles to each other, we end up with Metatron's Cube, and you might notice a curious overlap between this and a particularly interesting religion.

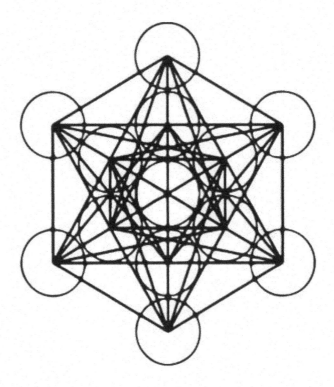

Through this pattern, we realize all perfect shapes - the shapes in three-dimensional space that have the same shape on each side. If the previous description was a bit too vague about a particular religion, let's highlight some important connections.

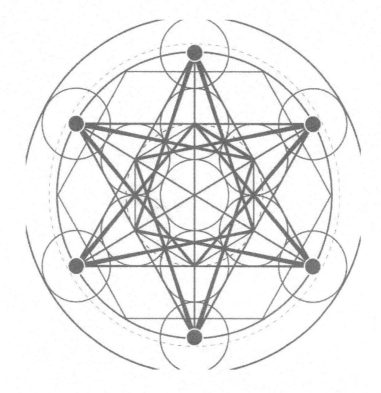

Through the philosophical understanding that the geometry of the universe is Divine, we end up at Jewish understanding.

A Short Conversation

The following is a conversational interpretation of a theory devised by Dr. Gerald Schroeder in his work, *The Science of God*

EMILY and Tyler are walking in an open field.

TYLER: What is an hour?

EMILY: A measurement of time.

TYLER: Sure, but what's it made of?

EMILY: Well, each hour is equally divided into 60 minutes, which are then divided into 60 seconds.

TYLER: But what makes up one second?

EMILY: Microseconds, nanoseconds, and even smaller parts of a second.

TYLER: But how do we know that? Like, scientifically, there's gotta be some way that we know one second is one second.

EMILY: There is.

TYLER: Oh, what is it?

EMILY: Quartz.

TYLER: The rock?

EMILY: Yeah, we know a few electrified quartz that releases a voltage, and if we add a small voltage to it, it vibrates. Scientists around the world agree that 32,768 of these vibrations is one second.

TYLER: So is that objectively one second?

EMILY: Kind of. Einstein's theory of special relativity doesn't allow for an objective viewpoint, so there is no such thing as an objective one-second length of time. Each viewpoint is equally subjective. A person in one place in space could feel a one-second length the same as a person in another place in space, but each of their timers would be different relative to the other. Special relativity established this understanding that spacetime bends and stretches. That stretching of the universe messes up any possible objective timescale.

TYLER: So, if there's no objective measurement of time, how do we know how old the universe is?

EMILY: Well, the terms "stretching" and "bending" may imply that the universe is bending more than it is. The universe, as a whole, is pretty flat, but we know there is an overall expansion of the universe, in that the wavelength of the cosmic background radiation, which originally was short, is now very long.

TYLER: So, if the universe is expanding, could we find where it began?

EMILY: No, the expansion of the universe is equal everywhere. We always think about expansion like it's filling up the available area, but each area of the universe is spreading apart from each other equally.

TYLER: Yesterday, you said that the universe was billions of years old. I think it was created in six days nearly 6000 years ago. Could special relativity and the expansion of the universe explain that it's both, in the same way that one second on one side of the universe is not the same as one second on the other side of the universe?

EMILY: Yes, it's possible to explain that the world could be created in six days nearly 6,000 years ago, but that timeline would need to be from a different perspective from our scientific consensus timeline of about 14 billion years, because the scientific timeline is from the perspective of Earth.

TYLER: Well, the six days would have to be from the perspective of objective truth. That's definitely outside of the Earthly viewpoint. Time-dilation is a little confusing. How long would each day have to be, if it's not exactly the length of a single Earth day?

EMILY: If each day wasn't exactly the length of one Earth day, it would have to be exponentially shorter than the previous day, especially if we're looking to match that Divine perspective to our current empirically-based historical understanding.

Day One would need to be about half of the length of universal existence, because that's how long it took for (a) light to break free from the universal mush and (b) star clusters to form galaxies.

Day Two would need to be about a quarter of all history, because that's about when the Earth was separated from the rest of the heavens.

Day Three would need to be a few billion years because that's how long it took for plant and microscopic creature life to develop.

Day Four would need to be one billion years because the Earth could finally see the sun, moon, and stars. The atmosphere cleared up and oxygen became prominent.

Day Five would need to be 500 million years, as the newly evolved marine animals take advantage of the oxygen-rich waters.

Day Six would need to be about 250 million years, as the massive extinction of nearly all other animals allows for mammals to reign supreme, eventually leading to humans. In total, these numbers roughly align with the scientific consensus theory of evolution.

TYLER: So, I can be religious and scientifically accurate?

EMILY: Yes, for the most part. Some denominations reject the idea that the six days were anything besides six Earth days, and that's OK for religion, but in terms of the empirical scientific process, this may be the best theory that fits with both scientific and religious understandings.

Free Will & Testament

Since, in Hasidism, free will actually is a derivative of our fundamental relationship with Hashem and the concept of Tzimtzum, we can therefore entertain a religious understanding of the expansion of the universe and what that means for the future of everything.

The expansion of the universe is Hashem continuously compacting Himself. It's a bit counterintuitive, but hear me out.

We understand that the universe is expanding because chromatically[4] near the creation of the universe, there was a ubiquitous background of electromagnetic waves perpetuating throughout the universe, a cosmic background radiation. Nowadays, we can measure the wavelength that perpetuated through the universe at that time by looking as far as telescopes can go and analyzing this background wall of radiation. Think about it like this: you take a flexible rope, put it on a tablecloth, and move it so it looks like a group of equally sized waves. If you condense the tablecloth, then the rope condenses and the size of each wave shrinks. If you stretch the tablecloth, each wave-length increases. So, if you analyze the wavelength of the cosmic background radiation and compare it to the size of each wave back at the creation of the universe, you can conclude that the universe is either shrinking, expanding, or not changing.

Lo and behold, it's a longer wavelength now than it was back then, indicating that the universe is stretching, and the difference in wave size between then and now indicates that the universe is expanding faster than the speed of light, but what does that mean for our Jewish understanding?

Well, an expansion that is faster than the speed of light means that from our perspective, distant objects in the night sky are slowly

---

[4] Related to time. "Near the creation" doesn't mean physically closer.

dimming, then disappearing. If we understand the creation of the universe to be a result of Hashem compacting Himself to allow for lower forms of life to exist, thereby dimming the originally-overwhelming universal light, then the natural understanding of the disappearance of distant objects can be reasonably understood to be the result of Hashem doing the process of tzimtzum in reverse through Divine expansion.

This explanation allows for a Jewish understanding of dark matter and dark energy, two seemingly-impossible entities that disproportionately increase the force of gravity. According to this reasoning and the understanding that Hashem is actively creating the universe, then it must be possible that Hashem stretches and bends the universe in such a way that (a) allows for our part of the universe to be relatively peaceful and (b) breaks our internal logic for trying to understand the universe without an omnipotent entity.

We can now discuss the complicated nature of free will.

Free Will

Free will, being a derivative of our fundamental relationship with Hashem and the concept of Tzimtzum, grants conscious beings the real choice of rejecting Godliness. From our understanding of tzimtzum, Hashem contracted Himself to allow for that decision, thereby granting the reality of not immediately seeing the consequence of one's relationship between oneself and Hashem.

This is fundamental to being human. For example, the part that makes a superhero story endearing is the superheroes' emphasizing their humanity even though they have the power of acting beyond. Superheroes have the free choice to act in the interest of humanity or against it. Choosing to act favorable to humanity was the defining characteristic of heroes, who would always fight against villains, individuals or entities that act against the interest of humanity.

The Crux of Xoot

More than just free will, religion, as a whole, is a lot like superheroes. Superheroes are considered fictional but they were not always designed to be entirely fictional.

This makes sense when you consider that the original superheroes were slightly embellished aspects of real people. Similarly, it's possible that the vast majority of world religions are at least somewhat unfaithful to the original (likely Jewish) version of their religion as modern superheroes are to their original (often Jewish) human source. Through the now-rapid advancements in science, religious leaders around the world have to constantly contend with the reality that their religious worldview may not align with modern scientific understanding. The same is true for denominations within Judaism that prioritize scientific understanding over most interpretations of Torah, but denominations within Judaism that prioritize most Jewish interpretations over modern science have mostly maintained the original source.

They are the continuation of the original people whose aspects were later embellished, translated, changed, reorganized, and reinterpreted millions of times over, establishing religions and influencing the history of the world.

Overall, the process of studying science in-depth is the unstoppable force from human logicality toward ultimate truth. The process of studying religion in-depth is analyzing an immovable object just before ultimate truth. When the unstoppable force meets this immovable object sometime in the future, our preparation may be the only thing that will keep us sane.

Kabbalah, through its Jewish mystical teachings, somehow reasoned the exact amount of layers of complexity within our universe, explaining the existential interactions between the layers of increasingly-complex Divine mercy (26) and the layers of increasingly-complex Divine-human connection (10), all done through the internally-consistent Judaic philosophical axioms in a grand effort to solve every seemingly-unanswerable question and the Qualia Paradox.

The Chabad denomination understands this perfectly, as they teach Kabbalistic philosophy to everyone. This act of unrestricted Kabbalistic teaching strikingly differs from the traditional Jewish modus operandi, unveiling a critical similarity between Jewish understanding and String Theory; one that inspired me to research more.

According to Hasidic Jewish understanding, the Divine connects to the highest possible level of human understanding, the highest dimension, through a substance very familiar to physics. The Creator is actively creating the world through Divine speech, which manifests in the world of human understanding through the movement of and interactions within this substance.

In Hebrew, this substance is called חוט.

In English, it is the humble string.

The Divine-human connection, the meaning of existence, sensible metaphysical solutions, and the pinnacle of modern physics are all based on fundamental strings.

Science answers how.

Judaism answers why.

Operating within the foundation of our preparation: aiding the maintenance of the sanity of mankind, kindling the light of our future perfection, and explaining the conquest of our understanding through number and measure can all be consequences of discovering the ultimate theory of everything.

That is Xoot.

"I love it when science eventually figures out what Jews already know; that fundamentally, everything is Torah".

Rebbetzin Rivka Rochel Liberow

IDEATION

Congratulations, you finished the book!

As a reward, please enjoy my personal, mostly unrelated conjectures about men & women in Judaism, evolution, aliens, and a bit of politics. Keep in mind, I do not have the expertise to justify these claims.

Men & Women

In Judaism, since the meaning of life is to enhance one's relationship with Hashem, men's and women's respective responsibilities are intricately tied to their natural tendency regarding this fundamental relationship.

Men are naturally less-adept at enhancing their relationship with Hashem without the use of stuff, so their responsibilities are defined through stuff, like wearing kippahs, tefillin, tzitzit, etc. Women are generally adept at enhancing relationships, so their fundamental relationship with the Divine is easier. Thus, women have fewer general responsibilities because they can be (and are) naturally closer to Hashem. Women, in Judaism, can be compared to a holier version of men that don't need stuff, that can deal with the abstract, and don't need the additional stuff-related boost in order to enhance the relationship emotionally.

Evolution-ish

Through the book of Bereshit (Genesis), we learn about two major transformative experiences: the punishment for eating from the fruit of knowledge and the experience that changed Yaakov's (Jacob's) name to Israel and resulted in the prohibition against eating rump roast because of the sciatic nerve. These two transformative actions are both the evolutionary result of human's differentiating themselves from animals. Our ability to be bipedal has the unfortunate side effects of childbirth pain and sciatica. Adam's punishment was the establishment of the need to farm; another action that differentiates us as humans from animals. Once humans moved beyond the need for everyone to be a farmer, humans cultivated the ability to reason and create.

Why Search For Aliens?

What are we really searching for? Are we searching for an animal that is less intelligent than humans? We have that on Earth. Are we searching for an entity that is more intelligent than humans? If that's the case, since Hasidic Judaism understands that there are two types of entities that are either the same level of existence or better than humans: angels and humans, and the difference lies in free-will. Angels are entities that are better than humans but have no free will. Humans have free will but are often worse than angels. If we want aliens to have no free will, then want to find angels in space. That's really cool, but I doubt it will happen. If we want aliens to have free will, just by looking at how humans have used their free will should give us a sense of what we should expect. Knowing about confirmed extraterrestrial life may be an infohazard such that if you knew about it, you would feel a sense of panic because it's only a matter of time before they destroy humanity, just like how humans subjugated the rest of the world's creatures. In this case, subjugation is equivalent to destruction.

Humans are the centerpiece of creation. I'm not contending that because of faith. Our conventional rules of physics govern everything the size of a quark and larger. Now, String Theory is a theory of everything and it's rooted in Judaism, but since (a) the quantum world can be analyzed to a depth twice as small to quarks as quarks are to the observable universe, and (b) the universe is larger than the observable universe (and as it expands, the understanding of universal scale breaks down), for the purposes of my point about scale, let's work with the conventional rules of physics, where the smallest thing that works with these rules is a quark and the largest thing is the observable universe.

If you were to lay out enough human brain cells to stretch across the observable universe, the number of quarks laid across a single brain cell would equal the same amount of brain cells laid across the observable universe.

Your thoughts are the center of the universe.

Government

The government runs on a flawed understanding that the means are justified by the ends, even when the means last forever because there are no ends. In politics, violence can be justified by a hopefully peaceful end, but the peaceful end is often ambiguously defined. From a political perspective, peace is relative, but metrics can be devised to test the level of objective peacefulness. If, in an objectively peaceful time, a powerful person finds that their area of the world is bad, then they feel justified to do violence and upend the ongoing peace. This may work on a relatively small scale because the peacefulness of a small neighborhood is easy to see, but a peacefulness on a nationwide and worldwide scale is much more ambiguous. The notion of the ends justifying the means works on a small scale, but a nationwide government should never accept a politically mandated complete destruction of a peaceful status quo because the act of mandating large changes in a peaceful status quo guarantees only the trials and tribulation, but not the peace and success.

The mirages on the horizon need only seem immediate for the trials to appear worthwhile.